the

BILLION DOLLAR PAPERCLIP

THINK SMARTER ABOUT YOUR DATA

the
BILLION
DOLLAR
PAPERCLIP

THINK SMARTER ABOUT YOUR DATA

GREGORY SHORT

MADELEINE

Published by Madeleine Books
www.MadeleineBooks.com

Cover and Interior Book Design by Monkey C Media
www.monkeycmedia.com

Edited by Derek Lewis

Printed in the United States of America

ISBN: 978-0-9897426-0-3 (Hard Cover); 978-0-9897426-1-0 (Soft Cover);
978-0-9897426-2-7 (e-Book); 978-0-9897426-3-4 (e-Pub)

Library of Congress Control Number: 2013918260

CONTENTS

PART II – THE FUNDAMENTALS OF CONTEXTUAL ANALYTICS

PART III – THE BUSINESS OF CONTEXTUAL ANALYTICS

PART I

THE NEED FOR CONTEXTUAL ANALYTICS

1

THE ROLE OF DATA IN YOUR COMPANY

Facts do not cease to exist because they are ignored.
—Aldous Huxley

Early in my career, a manager told me, "The four most impactful weeks you can get from an employee are the two after they first join and the two before they quit. In the first two weeks, they have fresh eyes and see everything that's wrong. Inspired, they're full of ideas and suggestions for change –but often unsure of how to enact it. By their last two weeks, they have become disillusioned. They see everything that's wrong with startling clarity. Bereft of hope that things could genuinely improve, they leave without telling management about the challenges the company faces. In between those four weeks, most employees are just cogs in the corporate machine."

I interact with these "cogs" inside the market research departments of companies every day. When I ask them how work is, they say, "Oh, you know—I do fire drill after fire drill, but my findings are ignored if they don't line up with what management wants to hear."

What a way to spend your career!

An air of futility permeates much of the work that market researchers do today. Some of the most important discoveries that emerge from their projects require their employers or clients to change key strategies or policies. As a result, they encounter substantial resistance. Change is not just scary—but hard—and almost always expensive.

No wonder executives like the status quo.

Let's look at it from management's perspective. Few executives want to believe that things under their leadership are moving in the wrong direction. Who wanted to believe that digital media would force many print publishers out of business, that cassette tapes (and now even CDs) would become obsolete, or that Asia would overtake Detroit in car manufacturing? The data pointing to these events should have naturally inspired fear. But who wants to present this kind of data to the board and be the harbinger of extinction? After all, many boards are only too willing to shoot the messenger.

But as Huxley said, ignoring the facts does not make them go away.

THE AGNOSTIC, THE OBSESSED AND THE AMBIVALENT

Before you can think smarter about your data, you have to first understand the role it currently plays inside your organization.

In business, we usually equate size with agility: smaller companies are seen as more nimble, quickly pivoting from one direction to another, while big companies are considered lumbering behemoths, slow to respond to the market. But this is a flawed assumption. Plenty of big companies have become adept at change and any number of smaller ones have proven unwilling to shift focus in the face of failure.

The data that corporate leaders need in order to anticipate change is often available to them. The difference is in the leaders' approach to the data. Those willing to face the fear-inducing reality of, "Sorry, boss—the data clearly shows that that consumers are moving from buying in-store to online," and change their strategy accordingly, are the ones who stay relevant in the ever-changing market.

Then again, sometimes it is not a lack of courage to face the research, but rather a lack of faith in it; that is, they are "data-agnostic." These types rarely trust what "the numbers" say, having been burned too many times. Who can blame them? Jump online and with a little digging you can find a statistic to support just about any "fact" or position you want to. Then, too, these types have sometimes misinterpreted data or even been victims of those who supplied them a flawed analysis. Their collective experiences led author Gregg Easterbrook to write, "Torture numbers, and they'll confess to anything." These managers have an understandable disdain for research, having learned to ignore the information and to just trust their gut.

While I can certainly sympathize, the data-agnostic poses an enormous danger. For instance, in 2011 the CEO of Netflix, Mr. Reed Hastings, announced that the company was going to spin off its DVD rental operations into a separate company, Qwikster, while Netflix continued to offer online video streaming. All Netflix customers would be forced to manage two accounts with two different subscriptions (at an overall higher rate) and two different product queues across two independent companies—in order to continue to have the exact same services they already enjoyed. Less than three hours after the announcement, customers posted over 17,000 comments on Netflix's website. Unsurprisingly, they were overwhelmingly negative. Facing the backlash of more than 800,000 account cancellations and a precipitous drop in their stock price, the company later reversed its decision.

In interviews after the debacle, Mr. Hastings said he was not sure whether the plan to split the company had ever been presented to customer focus groups before it was made public. He assumed it had been, but had no recollection what the research had indicated. For a company such as Netflix, known for being deeply data driven with their operations and technology, to act so inconsistently with the data underlying their business decisions was incredulous to observers.

To put a fine point on it: one data agnostic-decision nearly wiped out a billion-dollar company. That is the danger of having these types of managers and executives in positions where they can do serious damage.

On the other end of the spectrum you will find the "data-obsessed." Chris Anderson summed up their view in his quote, "With enough data, the numbers speak for themselves." They see data as Truth and Big Data as the Holy Grail. They want as many facts, statistics, and data points as possible. They do not question the data—they receive it, believe it, and execute against it. With these types, you find very little room for creative thought or instinctual decision-making. It can quickly lead to a case of paralysis by analysis, with too much time spent examining the data points while missing the bigger picture altogether.

You might think there is a Goldilocks moment where the middle of the two extremes is "just right." In my experience, this is worse. For the most part, the middle represents situational data users. That is, executives who use data as a façade to justify their current position.

They pay lip service to the numbers—because as a "rational" manager, that is what they are supposed to do—but in practice, the data is irrelevant, since they have already made up their minds to do whatever they want. Companies waste millions of market research dollars every year on such managers who surround themselves only with "yes men" and "yes data."

None of these approaches to data utilization will lead to long-term success for any organization. Data doesn't belong in the dungeon. Nor should data be ignored. And data should certainly not be put on a throne. But data *does* deserve a seat at the table.

GIVING DATA A SEAT AND A VOICE

What role does data play inside your organization today? Does it sit at the core of every major business decision? Or is it treated as a going-through-the-motions type of activity?

For the many companies operating in the rubber-stamp mentality, there is hope: the pendulum need not swing to the opposite side in order for productive change to occur. Simply put: companies do not need to be data-*driven* to be data-*enabled*.

As a CEO, I leverage numbers with the expertise of my staff to navigate my market. Otherwise, my company might wind up like so many other data-driven organizations, iterating themselves to death over reactive research findings. Companies that rely on data to the point that they forgo the value of human minds eventually die.

Yet when human minds become involved, there are other complications. In most meetings where change is required, there are winners and losers, disagreements, and common causes. The creative people rarely see eye to eye with sales or finance; the managers jockeying for promotion might succeed, or they might end up looking for new employment elsewhere. Politics often get in the way of data-enabled decision-making, a mistake that many junior leaders fall prey to. Strong leaders, on the other hand, attempt to avoid playing favorites by carefully weighing the merits of each person's argument by giving all sufficient gravity and voice, yet not so much that any one drowns out the others. Likewise, data should not be the ultimate solution that replaces the voices of everyone else, nor should it be constantly ignored.

Of course, just because a company is data-enabled does not make it an instant seer, going on to achieve market domination or always avoiding dangerous circumstances. Take Hurricane Sandy for example. In 2012, this "black swan" event brought New York City to a standstill. When New York allocated its public transportation budget, there was no data readily available to indicate that they should plan for something of that magnitude. In over a century of service, nothing on Sandy's scale had ever occurred. Similarly, no one predicted the Arab Spring because the events that occurred were historically unprecedented. No matter how appropriate of a role data plays, it cannot predict the unpredictable.

A data-enabled culture simply accords data its own voice. This approach recognizes that good research has its own value that should be weighed in the balance against other factors beyond the available data. In a data-enabled culture, information is effectively used to help companies ask better questions and make more informed decisions, without the polarizing influence of the data-obsessed or the data-agnostic. Data cannot be a crutch to replace good business instincts.

But neither can it be ignored or marginalized because it was misinterpreted or contradictory.

Just as it cannot be given too little weight, neither can it be given too much.

A Proven Approach

Once you understand the role of the data you use in your business, you can turn your focus to more interesting avenues of inquiry: "Why do we collect this data in the first place? Why choose some pieces of this dataset over others? How is the competition using this type of information?"

In my conversations with senior executives, they are often surprised when I point out that although they audit their inventory, processes and operations, finances, and human resources, they have never performed an audit on the information they use to make their business decisions. Such an audit can start with questions as simple as, "Where did this data come from? What does this data represent? What value are we expecting to extract from it? Are we actually extracting that value?"

I have been fortunate to witness firsthand the power data (or the lack thereof) can have. As what many would call a serial entrepreneur, I have founded a number of companies, ranging from consumer media and marketing, to software and education. My first start-up centered on helping people learn to utilize the internet during its infancy in the 1990s. Later, while finishing my law degree, I launched a number of other technology and media-related start-ups that I subsequently sold to such companies as the Hearst Corporation and Sony.

It was as a result of my transaction with Sony that I was afforded the opportunity to work inside their organization for a number of years. There, I got first-hand experience with the difficulties the largest developers and publishers of interactive media were facing. The most significant of these challenges posed a very real threat to the stability of the multibillion-dollar interactive entertainment industry: there was no efficient and reliable way to get the necessary information to make data-enabled decisions.

I set out to change that.

In 2006, I founded Electronic Entertainment Design and Research (EEDAR) alongside Geoffrey Zatkin, a longtime friend and veteran game designer. Since the company began offering commercial services in 2008, EEDAR has become the largest market research and consulting firm in the world for the interactive entertainment industry.

Video games are a big business. They generate more money each year than Hollywood and are consumed by hundreds of millions of people across the entire globe. The industry is also challenging. Video games have one of the highest new product introduction rates of any market with thousands of new games released each month. There is enormous fragmentation in the supply chain, only getting worse as more devices and technology platforms emerge. Manufacturers and data suppliers are infamous for their highly competitive and secretive natures. The technology ecosystem that drives the industry evolves daily, facing constantly changing demographics and consumption habits. Yet despite all these obstacles, EEDAR has been able to not only thrive but to catalyze market research vendors, buyers, and consumers to work toward a truly data-enabled community. Insights that researchers and analysts used to only dream about are now possible because of the framework and data ecosystem EEDAR pioneered.

The astounding ability of this approach is the ease by which it helps to answer the most critical of business questions: "Why?"

More than just a methodology, it goes far beyond the limited rewards of traditional data synthesis to extract exponential value from disparate datasets. As the amount of data available to market researchers grows, there must also come an evolution in business intelligence and consumer insights.

I call this methodology "Contextual Analytics."

If a fragmented, data-dysfunctional industry like interactive entertainment can be transformed not only into a data-enabled community, but one that embraces an entirely new approach to market research altogether...

...yours can, too.

.

2

CONTEXT IS EVERYTHING

If content is king, context is its crown.
—Eric Schmidt, former CEO of Google

On September 24, 2012, an NFL referee raised his hands and unleashed Armageddon.

Correction: a *replacement* referee raised his hands, since the actual NFL referees were on strike.

The Green Bay Packers were leading against the Seattle Seahawks. Seahawks player Golden Tate went up to catch a pass that, if successful, would immediately result in a touchdown for his team. Then, Packers safety M.D. Jennings intercepted the ball. Video footage later clearly revealed that at no time did Tate have the ball in his possession. It was a clear interception for Green Bay.

After the interception, two replacement referees ran over to make their calls. One began to raise his hands as if to signal a clock stoppage and a touchback. But as he did so, the other quickly threw his arms up to signal a touchdown. After a quick conversation, they let the touchdown call stand. By NFL rules, once a simultaneous catch rule is issued, it can't be reviewed again.

After watching the replays, there was little doubt as to what really happened. Even fans who hated Green Bay felt the team had been robbed. The Seahawks went on to win 14-12.

Fans from both sides unleashed their fury and Twitter (among other websites) exploded. Immediately afterward and for the next twenty-four hours, it seemed like everyone from around the world posted tweets about the stupidity of the NFL, the referee lockout, the game stolen by the Seahawks, and the injustice done to the Green Bay Packers.

With this event in mind, imagine if two years later analysts perform market research for the NFL on Twitter-related activity. In doing so, they come across an outlier: a disproportionately large surge in NFL-related tweets from September 24 and 25. When they run that surge against TV ratings, they see no correlation between it and the subsequent number of TV viewers. This is odd because everywhere else in their model a surge in Twitter activity correlates with an increase in viewership for the following game. Before this outlier, they predicted that a disproportionately large amount of Twitter activity would result in a disproportionately large numbers of viewers, but September 24 broke their model. You can imagine them sitting around the table, scratching their heads, and trying to explain the oddity.

Of course, as soon as someone jumps on the internet and searches for "NFL 9/24/2012" they will quickly see that the uptick in tweets was an angry backlash against the NFL. With a little more digging, they might find that NFL fans decided to go on strike until the replacement refs were thrown out and the actual refs brought back in. All of a sudden, the outlier makes sense—

...*because it was put into context.*

On the other hand, if the same team were to perform the same analysis for NASCAR, they might find a macabre twist. Once again, they would likely find that the more positive NASCAR-related tweets posted, the more viewership increases thereafter—but with a surge in negative tweets, viewership increases exponentially. Why? Because surges in negative NASCAR tweets often revolve around accidents, injuries, and sometimes death. With the heightened drama, NASCAR fans might be even more engaged, holding their breath to see if this race will have a disastrous wreck like the one last week. Their behavior mirrors what you see when there is a wreck on the highway: everyone "rubbernecks" to see what happened.

The bottom line is that when data is viewed in isolation, absent of context, it is next to impossible to truly know everything that single piece of information could be telling them.

How Contextual Analytics Mirrors the Brain

Our brains constantly contextualize the world around us. From finding patterns in foods we like to predicting our significant others' behavior, our brains are always forming new synapses to link different thoughts, memories, feelings, sensations, and reactions to everything. When sci-fi movies represent these linkages, they often show a web-like network of neural patterns with millions of strands connecting the nodes.

Contextual analytics is a natural extension of what we already do every second of every day. It is an attempt to reproduce the human brain's neural network with data and technology—to find ways to logically link isolated data to arrive at a greater understanding of the whole story. While I believe that the adoption of contextual analytics is revolutionary for the market research industry, when we look at it from the bigger picture, we see it is not that revolutionary at all. It just so happens that the systems, tools, and technology are finally catching up to what our species has done for millennia.

In his famous work *Thinking, Fast and Slow*, Nobel Prize winner for economics Dr. Daniel Kahneman explored the brain's two states in attempting to deal with the decisions it faces in everyday life. In explaining the way we think, he breaks thought into two systems. System 1 is fast, intuitive, emotional, and capable of multiple decisions at the same time (not all of them correct). System 2 is slower, more deliberative, and logic-driven. Unfortunately, the majority of business decisions are made using System 1, while the majority of market research approaches today attempt to replicate System 2. There is a chasm that often leads to frustration or lack of engagement with what the research can show as a result. So how does contextual analytics solve this problem?

The real challenge with addressing data today is not that we do not have enough of it. We have plenty of data. In fact, we have far more data right now than anyone practically knows what to do with, and more of it is collected every day. The problem is that we do not know how to make it work together. According to Jeff Kaplan, managing director of THINK Strategies, "Big data isn't the solution. The solution is having the right set of tools to properly slice and dice the data."

Our brains have similar problems. In *Successful Remembering and Successful Forgetting*, Aaron Benjamin compiled a range of studies related to how brain memory functions, based on principles theorized by Robert Bjork. One of the most interesting findings of these studies is that the human brain never actually forgets anything. That is right: it is not the memory that decays. Rather, it is the ability to recall that memory that becomes challenged. As we get older and add layer upon layer of memory into our synapses, older and less used memories become akin to worn out dirt pathways overgrown with weeds. But the brain is an amazing thing: it actually builds more effective memory recall systems as we re-establish these pathways regarding things that have been 'forgotten'.

In an attempt to optimize our recall ability and to slice and dice our memories into useful information, our brains naturally create relationships between memories in an attempt to organize the billions of pieces of information rolling around up there. We cannot stop these organic associations, even if we wanted to. Even the beloved sci-fi character Dr. Who remarked on this canny aspect of our species: "I love humans. Always seeing patterns in things that aren't there."

It is true enough: with no effort, our brains automatically sort, sift, and try to make sense of everything we know in an attempt to continually learn so that we do not make repeated mistakes, improve in our innate ability to predict outcomes, and change our behavior early enough so future actions result in more optimal outcomes.

It is a good thing they do. How often are we about to do something and suddenly remember a colossal mistake we made under an entirely different set of circumstances? How often do we take lessons that we learned in an unrelated scenario and successfully apply them to a brand new situation? When we learn a principle or moral, all we have done is create metadata around the reality we experienced. Our brain somehow connects two seemingly unrelated dots, but in doing so it dumps a wealth of experience and insight onto the problem at hand.

Imagine if companies could do this proactively. What if they could link databases so unrelated that all they had in common was the slenderest of threads…and yet in doing so were able to bring an enormous amount of data that preempted a potentially disastrous design decision? What if enough disparate datasets were associated together to deliver clear explanations as to why specific market trends and consumer behaviors were occurring?

Contextual analytics is an inspired notion: Shouldn't we *consciously* enable our information ecosystems to do what we have been *unconsciously* doing with our brains all this time?

TRADITIONAL RESEARCH METHODS

Before we explore how to create these new ecosystems, let's take a moment to talk about the main types of market research methods in use today.

Qualitative research generally involves working with small groups or individuals to understand the thought process and motivations behind decisions. By nature, it generally involves open-ended questions that produce a lot of "unstructured data"; or simply, sentences of text related to the topic of inquiry. These are often done at the beginning of a research project to help refine the scope and direction of future efforts.

Quantitative research utilizes a stricter approach of asking explicit questions against a population (either a whole or partial sample). The responses to these can then be analyzed using traditional statistical approaches. For example, utilizing surveys and polls to answer questions should build up a sufficient amount of information to then analyze for insights. This is where the majority of research has been historically conducted.

Predictive analytics applies mathematical formulas or algorithms against collections of qualitative, quantitative, and other relevant data to spot trends to predict future behavior. Perhaps the industry that uses this most aggressively is the stock market where every second hundreds of different algorithms are actively trading securities on behalf of their human counterparts. Predictive analytics is the underpinning of most technology businesses trying to leverage data in a commercial way. From recommended videos on Netflix or Amazon, to how airfare tickets are dynamically priced by airlines, predictive analytics has been at the epicenter of the Big Data boom.

Of course there are other types of research methodologies. Qualitative research alone can be performed in dozens of ways from focus tests, to one-on-one interviews, to consumer shadowing and more. Conjoint analysis utilizes a combination of methods to gauge the factors influencing decisions by presenting a series of questions with slight variations. The list of available approaches and techniques goes on. The common challenge of all these "tools" available to market researchers is that none easily solve some fundamental problems.

WHY THESE METHODS TELL ONLY PART OF THE STORY

To demonstrate their shortcomings, let's look at a practical, everyday question that data should provide the answer to. Let's imagine we are at a product planning meeting for an office supply company. The CMO wants to know, "What month is going to be best for us to launch our latest glow-in-the-dark paperclip?" The company hires a market research firm who returns with a very impressive PowerPoint that is summed up in one word: "April."

But how did the market research firm get to that answer?

They may have started with a qualitative discussion group and deduced that shortly before taxes are due on April 15th there is a huge need for paperclips. They passed this finding along to their quantitative group who took the hypothesis and conducted a survey of 500 average American taxpayers. The group validates the hypothesis with the "discovery" that 95% of respondents purchase paperclips in that month. The predictive analytics team then leveraged data on historical paperclip sales—some of it purchased from a measurement provider, some of it from their internal figures—and performed regressions against historical sales for new product launches. From that, they determined that March and April are indeed the two months where the largest sales of paperclip-related products occur during a typical year.

The above approach is almost stock standard for market research. Each method provided some interesting pieces to a larger understanding of market opportunity. A key problem with the above approach is its heavy reliance on the scientific method. The testing of the early hypothesis ("Is April a good month to launch a new paperclip?") focused the researchers' attention along specific lines of inquiry. But in doing so, they may have completely missed more important discoveries.

Did they factor in that this paperclip glows in the dark? Did they look at how many other new products will launch at the same time? Are most of those new products temporary repackaging of existing inventory, bundled products as part of a "tax pack," or are they something truly new? So many questions remain unanswered, despite the expensive research performed.

Or what if Pepsi wanted to know why some consumers choose Coke over their products? They might commission a research firm to "go find out why those people like to drink Coke more than Pepsi." The analysts would create a questionnaire listing all the conceivable reasons someone might enjoy Coke more than Pepsi: fizzier, less bubbly, sweeter, more filling, less syrupy, and so on. But in doing so, they are neglecting to ask a better question. Instead of asking why consumers *like* Coke over Pepsi, they should ask why consumers *purchase* Coke over Pepsi.

The fact may be that many people buy Coke for a completely different reason than their liquid properties. Maybe Coke does a better job merchandising in local stores, or runs better pricing promotions. It could be a consumer liked the recent advertisement for Coke on television, or that they think the Santa Claus can is cute during the holidays. If analysts begin their research with the assumption that cola sodas are bought solely on the basis of flavor preference, they might miss the other facts that impact their profits.

Herein lies the heart of the problem: a traditional analytic approach almost always acts on specific questions to pursue insights. Unfortunately, the questions usually come from the people commissioning the project who believe they already know the answer. In other words, the majority of market research today is tainted before it even begins by pursuing the answer to a hypothesis at the exclusion of other lines of inquiry.

Cue contextual analytics.

Contextual Analytics

It was never a career goal of mine to become a pioneer of contextual analytics. Rather, I was simply trying to help companies make decisions that balanced their creative intuition with real supporting data. At some point in working with all the data that had been amassed, though, certain odd data points became noticeable that lay completely outside of any kind of predictive model, much like the hypothetical NFL Twitter researchers earlier. For instance, one game might sell successfully, but an almost identical one released a few weeks later might not sell at all.

Isaac Asimov once said, "The most exciting phrase to hear in science, the one that heralds new discoveries, is not 'Eureka!' but 'That's funny...'"

Essentially, that is what happened at EEDAR. We began asking, "Why?" As in, "Why was this game a spectacular success, earning millions of dollars, while its nearly identical competitor was a spectacular failure?"

We began with the obvious: how much did different game companies spend on marketing and how did this affect the success of individual products? This little bit of data did not reveal much. Some companies spent relatively little and still met with success, while others spent a small fortune and went bust. Obviously, the answer went beyond just how big their marketing budget was. So we went a layer deeper: where did they spend their advertising dollars—internet, TV, magazines, radio, or elsewhere?

It seemed logical to extend our investigation a little further to ask what the actual ads were. Did the internet advertising dollars go toward game trailers, banner ads, or something else? What magazines did ads appear in? Did the TV ads appear at primetime or during the 2 a.m. infomercial slots?

The deeper we drilled, the more we began to see what worked and what did not. Certain media provided a high return on marketing dollars spent. Games positioned one way vastly outperformed those positioned another way. Once we identified the elements that made significant impact, we began to share our insights with development companies. They would ask whether option A or option B was best. Of course, the answer was, "It depends. In one context, it's A, but in another context it's B." We could deliver the exact answer they needed, but only after we established the parameters—that is, the context—of their question.

Compare this scene to many other major research firms. When a client asks them how much money they can expect to make, the firm plots a simple line graph. On the X axis is how much money the industry spends on average; on the Y-axis, how much is grossed. Draw a line through that, find out how much the client plans to spend on the X-axis, and then see what the corresponding Y-value is: "Well, there it is: if you spend that much, you can expect to make this much—more or less."

A traditional analytics approach takes into account just a handful of data measurement pieces that deliver broad answers to broad questions. Contextual analytics, on the other hand, offers a far more powerful set of tools because it takes into account ten, twenty, or even a hundred factors that have been shown to affect the success of a product. Instead of predicting how much money a company can expect to make on their product (the broader the question, the broader the range), we can tell them how much money they can expect to make within a specific set of circumstances; the more specific the parameters, the more specific the figure. The more identified elements of success they incorporate into their product, the more success they can expect to have.

At EEDAR, the company's services have become increasingly accurate as more types of data are brought into the contextual ecosystem. Sales forecasts provided for clients are now generally within 10% of actual performance over 85% of the time. This may not seem that amazing… until you consider that many of those forecasts are produced before a product has even begun production. Such accuracy has saved millions of dollars in what might otherwise have been miss-allocated development efforts.

Even more remarkable is that the data can precisely show what factors will drive the forecast up or down. Contextual analysis does not just produce sales estimates. It also supplies guidance towards optimal product characteristics derived from numerous sources of information to improve potential for success in the market.

The Underpinning of Contextual Analytics

But it takes more work than just having a lot of datasets at your disposal to achieve these kinds of insights. The fundamental keys to a successful contextual analysis—as well as the fundamental challenge—are quality attribution and identity datasets.

That is, sets of rich metadata that can all work together.

Simply put, metadata describes data. The metadata about a website might comprise when the site was published, what type of website it is (blog vs. ecommerce), when it was last updated, how many words it contains, who wrote it, and even a short description of what the site says. While these fields are determined by the author of the website, search engines might add additional metadata to determine search engine optimization, such as what the key search terms should be. Over time the search engines can build up measurement data related to the metadata as well: how often is the site updated, how many people have shared it, and through what different methods have they done so? Notice that none of these fields or values have anything to do with the actual content of the website itself. It could be about the Kentucky Derby or cybernetics. While the content of either site radically differs, both end up with consistent attribute fields (or metadata) that can unlock new information and allow new perspectives on each respective site.

Tracking those attributes makes it easy to compare the two. If a market research team wants to determine how to get more people to share online content via social media for blogs, they can use the metadata to isolate the set of relevant sites and then use the collected measurement data to search for insights. After holding constant the key search terms, date of publication, and page ranks, the analysts may find that how frequently the site is updated correlates with high social media shares.

While this might be common sense (the more that the site provides fresh information, the more that people share that information), being able to rank the sites by key search terms could reveal different behaviors. Perhaps media-related websites immediately generate higher social media shares, but hobby-related websites generate more social media shares over a sustained period. The insight would be that many people interact with a media page but do so quickly, never to return again. On the other hand, fewer people interact with a hobby-related page, but they do so over and over again.

This knowledge would be golden to an online advertiser. It would mean that their ad campaign would become quickly ineffective on a media site, but it would stay in front of another audience for a longer period on a hobby site. They should buy ads from the appropriate site based on whether they are doing a limited time promotion or a longer-term brand building exercise. This insight could not be possible without a solid layer of attribution data.

The more context analysts have, the more of a nuanced analysis they can provide.

You Can't Track It If You Can't See It

It is relatively easy to track the attributes of digital content; it is much harder with physical products. Take books, for instance. While comparable to websites in function—they both deliver information— they are incomparable to websites in how easy it is to fill in the blank attributes. The publishing industry groups books by categories and subcategories. Walk into any given bookstore and you will find a romance section, a sci-fi/fantasy section, a business section, a children's section, and so forth. Some sections are divided into sub-sections, such as an entrepreneurship shelf within the business aisle. An individual bookstore may track sales by item and by category, but it cannot see much further than that. If an individual book or author sells well, they may order more of the title or the series. If an overall category does well, the bookseller may allocate more shelf space to it, such as eliminating some home improvement magazines in order to stock an increased number of fashion magazines.

Without knowing the attributes of the individual products though, the bookseller cannot optimize the products for its customers. There may be a hidden relationship between the number of best-selling books that is not readily apparent from looking at the cover. Most romance books have the same guy and girl on the cover, and most have a laughably identical plot: guy meets girl, guy chases girl, guy finally gets girl, and they live happily ever after. The metadata for a number of romance novels might have the author, publisher, date of publication, and a few other items.

But what if they had a field that said what time period the book was set in? And what if they had an attribution field that said whether or not time travel was involved? With these two key pieces of data, the buyer for the bookstore might discover that romances with a time-traveling heroine set in the Scottish Highlands in the 1800s were outperforming all other romance novels five-to-one. Such information would be staring them right in the face—if only they had the attribution layer there to show it. Could the buyer use such information to make more money?

Absolutely!

A solid undergirding of attribution drives contextual insights and reveals the previously hidden linkages to other products. Once the bookstore manager sees Scottish time-traveling romances selling, they could cross-merchandise their display with a similar time-traveling science-fiction novel that included romance. While the two genres are generally on opposite sides of the store, the person who bought a romance book that included a little sci-fi might very well buy a sci-fi book that included a little romance—if the two books are close enough. But until the bookseller finds that one data point in common, those potential sales will never be realized; their readers will go elsewhere to buy other time-traveling romances set in the Scottish Highlands.

Imagine being able to do that on a global scale, cross-selling transmedia entertainment or leveraging a licensed sports brand across multiple products. We have just begun to tap into the multibillion-dollar potential of gluing products' attribution sets together to see what opportunities are staring us right in the face.

3

WHAT'S YOUR DATA HIDING?

Everything we hear is an opinion, not a fact.
Everything we see is a perspective, not the truth.
—MARCUS AURELIUS

A paperclip.

An innocuous little thing. Any office has hundreds—if not thousands—lying around, although no one gives them a second thought. They are so common as to be invisible; there is a handful in almost every office drawer, on every conference table, and underneath every desk. No one even notices a paperclip until they need to keep some papers together. Yet the processes and industries involved in transforming the paperclip from idea to everyday office supply product easily surpass a billion dollars.

That's right: the billion dollar paperclip.

A paperclip's journey begins deep underground. The process to transform raw ore into a finished product touches property rights, mining, heavy machinery, smelting, extrusion, logistics and eighteen-wheelers, unions, engineers, the patent office, insurance, OSHA, robotics, and myriad other extraction and manufacturing activities.

Of course, after the paperclip is manufactured it still needs to be sold. The retail process spans consumer insights, cardboard packaging, customer relationship management software, leases, utility companies, the fire code, minimum wage, janitorial services, interior design, and thousands of other variables—just to get it on the shelf. That is, unless it is offered online, in which case it would involve servers, web design, graphic artists, software testers, warehouses, and a customer service center.

Then, of course, it needs to get off the shelf and into the hands of a customer. Luring you into the store or onto the website might come in the form of direct mail (involving stamps, postage meters, mail trucks, the entire paper industry, and tracking whether it was mailed to your home or office), an emailed coupon (involving a customer sign-up service, the marketing department, how they got your email in the first place, an IT policies and procedures manual, the Taiwanese factory making the wireless modem), a newspaper ad (involving a number of English and journalism degrees, the entire ink industry, whether you saw it on a weekend or weekday, whether you are a subscriber or an occasional reader), or a product promotion bundle (involving the entire upstream manufacturing process for the other product, the operations and marketing departments of the suppliers as well as the retailers, the process of the adhesive used to glue the coupon onto the box of paperclips, whether it was placed on an end cap or by the cash register, what other products were sitting on the shelf beside it).

You might have seen the retailer's promotion on TV (involving FTC licenses, tracking which channel or channels you saw it on, the manufacture of cable wire, the refinement of the liquid crystals, the quality of the broadcast, the construction crew that built the TV station) or heard it on the radio (involving the manufacturer of your car, what time of the day the ad aired, how often it aired, where you physically were when you heard it). And of course, after you use the paperclip it will eventually end up recycled, or in a landfill, both of which have their own litany of associated activities.

The list of every process, product, or service that goes into the manufacture and sale of a single paperclip is virtually endless.

If a simple paperclip represents a billion-dollar ecosystem, imagine the case for more complex products such as mobile phones, computers, or cars. I use a paperclip in the example above, but the product at hand does not matter. The paperclip is merely a metaphor representing the products and services that we all work with on a day-to-day basis. Whether you work with video games or violins, packaged goods or pharmaceuticals, it is a simple truth that no aspect of any product lives in isolation. There is always a deeper story of interconnected activities that, if linked together, enable a contextualized view of everything behind it and beyond it. But despite this mind-bending perspective, most executives focus on the myopic. They look at how many paperclips sold this quarter, compare it to how many were sold last quarter, declare it "good" or "bad," and go on with business as usual.

Look at everything they've missed!

WHY? WHY? WHY?

If the office supply store does not know how or why you came to be standing in their paperclip aisle, then they have absolutely no clue how to get you to come in again. They throw money into marketing and advertising, and then pray it somehow reaches you. But without a means to collect the data around why you chose their store for your purchase, how can they ever know how to improve their marketing tactics in the future?

This true-to-life example provides an accurate analogy for the business of market research. It is easy for a company to observe certain kinds of human behavior, such as when sales plummet or a new product begins flying off the shelves. Often, competitors see this success and quickly create me-too products in an attempt to cash in on the latest craze. Consumers are happy because there are plenty of gadgets to go around and companies are happy because there is plenty of money to go around. Everybody wins. Right?

The reason I have a job is because, more often than not, the exact opposite is true. Competitors release me-too toys that never sell. Companies try to build on their own previous success and waste millions of dollars designing and developing products that suddenly no one wants. But until they know why, they will continue to pour money down a black hole.

Why? Why were people fighting over Beanie Babies in the 90s but now you cannot give them away? Why was one action movie a blockbuster while another one just like it did not break even? Why did predecessors similar to the iPhone never catch on but Apple's device revolutionized multiple industries? Why, why, *why?*

Research professionals seek to answer that question every day. Companies constantly poll their customers to understand what influences them to do one thing over another: at restaurants ("What brings you in today?"), on websites ("How did you hear about us?"), and on the phone ("What's the reason for your call?").

"Why?" is the billion-dollar question.

LITTLE OR NO CHANGE SINCE THE DARK AGES

Questions such as these have been the core of market research for decades now—most often pursued by qualitative or quantitative methodologies. Until the last few years, businesses did not have many options when it came to observing and measuring human behavior. It was surveys or nothing. Consequently, survey-based approaches dominated the industry. Even today, in the age of Big Data, it is not an exaggeration to say that survey and group-based data collection activities represent over 60% of all market research dollars spent. That is an astonishing figure when you take into account all the other methods researchers now have at their disposal.

An embarrassing problem for today's market research industry is that it has changed little since the last major revolution when the advent of consumer-accessible computing allowed for analyzing amounts of data previously unimaginable.

Some of the first people to deal with computer-based data analysis were insurance actuaries. These people were essentially statisticians who used census data and insurance claim data to predict life expectancy and corresponding risk. They were among the first to spot the link between smoking and shorter life expectancy, and thus the difference in insurance premiums for smokers. By moving away from their paper-laden systems to computer processing, they were able to cover a much wider range of risk categories with higher accuracy than ever before.

Such types of analyses were radical advancements in market research at the time. Unfortunately, the industry has not progressed much since. Yes, the researchers have newer tools and faster computers, but the basic approach to data collection remains unchanged. Instead of mailed questionnaires, we have emailed questionnaires; in place of in-store surveys, we have online surveys. Instead of reams of punch cards, we have software spreadsheets.

This is not entirely the research industry's fault. Until recently, we had little syndicated measurement data readily available. On the supply side, companies had a record of how much they sold to their distributors and consumers. They might commission a research firm to track product sales against advertising campaigns. But there was very little granular data.

Today, of course, that has changed. The average American's cable box provides a wealth of information. Automobile manufacturers can collect data about drivers' habits via the onboard system, uploaded when hooked up to a diagnostic tool during an oil change. Imagine the wealth of information this provides cable companies or car designers. If cable companies know that enough people watch both NBA and NHL, they can offer an incentivized package targeted just to those consumers who like to flip between the two. Or Cadillac might discover that Escalade drivers go too long between oil changes and find a way to encourage better maintenance, leading to more overall product satisfaction and service revenue.

But again…if your company limits its "research efforts" to reporting sales figures and buying datasets here and there, are you really getting all the insights you need?

Where We Can Go From Here

Political campaigns often act on faulty logic. If a poll shows a candidate down by a few points among rural Iowa voters whose primary concern is healthcare, the candidate might break out their overalls and give a series of speeches for or against any particular version of healthcare. But what they may miss is that Iowa farmers are more concerned about healthcare because decreases to their farming subsidies have now created budget constraints that make healthcare a more glaring expense for them. They might not care about healthcare if they had more money in their pockets. As such, they scratch their heads as whatever hopeful candidate talks to them about the symptom (healthcare) while missing the disease (income).

This disconnect between the real issues and the statistics are often the reason so many people feel that the numbers have little relevance in their lives. When the root cause of an issue isn't explicitly connected to a data point, decision-makers draw their own conclusions about why the number is what it is. The leaders try to answer the wrong questions and fix the wrong problem.

Very little in this chapter comes as a shock or surprise to anyone in the market research business. Everyone realizes that limitations exist, surveys have flaws, and studies are appropriated for individuals' own agendas. Were there no other options, the way it has been would still be the only way forward. Fortunately, there is a better one.

This alternate approach does not eliminate the need for the existing methods of collecting data or performing research. The results they produce are necessary as a foundation for where the market is being driven.

The destination? That's right: contextual analytics.

A bold claim, I know. But as you read through the rest of this book and see the potential it offers, it will become very clear why this approach represents the inevitable—and incredibly rich—future of business intelligence.

4

BEYOND BIG DATA

Tradition: just because you've always done it that way
doesn't mean it's not incredibly stupid.

—Despair.com

"Will you milk my cow?"

Anyone who has ever been on Facebook has received some kind of request along these lines. FarmVille was one of the most popular online social games of all time, drawing millions of users into its virtual world. But after a time its developer, Zynga, steadily lost both users and consumer popularity across a number of its games, despite the company's stock offering ranking as one of the largest technology IPOs in history, valuing the company at over $7 billion.

Why?

Some industry insiders point to a lack of innovation, to copying other games, or simply to riding a dying fad to the ground. Any of those may be true and a significant contributor. However, Zynga's Achilles heel might not be that there was too little innovation—it could be there was too much.

Zynga tested iteration after iteration after iteration to see what resulted in the most sales: "Does this screen lead to more engagement and in-app purchases or does that one? Should the notifications pop up more often or less? What types of actions or items make the players invite the most friends to come play online?"

The decisions of which iterations to push out to everyone were largely computer driven, and mostly based on A/B tests to see which version resulted in more money. Their theory was basically, "The more that people buy, they more that they must be enjoying what they're doing."

The company amassed a staggering amount of data on in-game player behavior, so much so that they could make a change for just a small sample of players and gather enough feedback to confidently decide whether to roll the change out to the other 99%.

Zynga definitely had Big Data.

What Zynga did not have was a contextual understanding of their user base, nor the qualitative aspects of their games. They could say with certainty that a particular change resulted in more immediate sales, but they could not definitively say why. They could not say whether such changes increased or decreased a players' overall enjoyment, nor whether they were telling their friends about it (outside of linked social media notifications like Facebook). Once their user base began to dwindle, they had no data to indicate what was wrong. They could not tell whether their former players switched to other games on their mobile phones, switched to other gaming platforms, or decided to give up on games altogether and started reading *Ulysses*. No one at Zynga knew.

Zynga was incredibly successful at monetizing their players. Their data scientists were disproportionately determining game design instead of actual game designers. Not surprisingly, allowing the math to take the lead undermined the most fundamental principles of any entertainment experience: fun. Over time, people who had spent significant sums of money on their games began maturing into a "once bitten, twice shy" mentality. Despite the evolutionary advancements in Zynga's leading games, former fans quickly headed for the exits. The core of Zynga's mathematical approach did not allow for significantly new or innovative experiences.

Despite all the information at their fingertips, Zynga backed themselves into a corner—and Big Data couldn't tell them where to go.

"Big" Only Means More of the Same

Don't be misled. Big Data is still the "next big thing."

MIT professor Michael Stonebraker said it like this: "It is interesting to note that a substantial subset of the computer science community has redefined their research agenda to fit under the marketing banner of 'Big Data.' As such, it is clearly the 'buzzword du jour.'"

Across many industries, people are rushing to collect data, stick it in an algorithm, and then sit back and let Truth rise to the surface. With enormous data samples, they inevitably find some interesting things that snap, crackle, and pop.

But the only way to get the real story out of one dataset is to align it with other datasets. The more datasets that are aligned, the richer the picture that can be painted. From a market research perspective, reality is a fragmented jigsaw puzzle (minus the box with a picture); market data provides different pieces of the puzzle. The more pieces a researcher finds, the more clearly they can see what is going on in isolated areas. Given enough time, they can soon get an idea of what the big picture looks like, even if they are still missing some pieces here and there.

One of Big Data's challenges is that despite representing an overwhelming amount of information, it is almost always limited to just one type of data. With Zynga, an A/B test would return which new in-game gizmo resulted in more clicks, but what about the rest of the story? Game engineers could not tell if the very players they measured decided five minutes later that they had had enough and swore off FarmVille altogether. Unless and until the game designers gathered a different type of data, they could only make decisions based on the isolated data available—isolated despite representing millions of players and billions of interactions.

One type of data represents only one piece of the puzzle.

If a researcher collects a massive amount of gameplay behavior, the researchers can zoom in on that puzzle piece. They can whip out an electron microscope and see the very atoms of that single aspect. They can discern what the piece is made of, what kind of cardboard it was printed on, and exactly where the printing pigments came from. But regardless of how much they understand about that one piece, at the end of the day, it is still just a one small component of the entire puzzle. Until another piece is found, all the decisions made will be based on $1/1,000^{th}$ of the big picture.

That's not much.

How Contextual Analytics Fills the Gaps

When most people talk about Big Data, 95% of the time they talk about very deep data in one industry segment or very thin data across a number of industry segments.

Visa has information on billions upon billions of credit card transactions. From data mining, Visa can provide very accurate profiles of different demographics, predict the economic conditions of certain geographies, and paint a comprehensive pictures of an individual cardholder's life. Visa knows the businesses where the cardholder spent money, what industry each business is in, how much the cardholder spent, and how likely they are to do it again. It has very thin data but spread across an impressive array of industry verticals and populations.

What Visa does not know is what, specifically, its cardholders buy.

Vons, a chain of grocery stores in southern California, on the other hand, knows only what occurs in its own stores. (Technically, Vons merged with Safeway, but let's use them as a proxy for any regional chain.) If you spend $9,000 on wine and beer at Vons, all Visa can see that is that you spent nine grand at a grocery store; therefore, an analysis would reveal that you spent nine grand on groceries. Vons knows that you spent $9,000 on beer and wine but has no idea where else you buy your booze (or anything else). One company knows all the places where you shop and how much you spend; the other knows exactly what you bought in their store, but nothing more. One's data is broad and thin while the other's is narrow and deep. Independently, both companies' collective datasets could reveal million-dollar insights into consumer behavior, but linking them together could yield billion-dollar insights.

So Big Data by itself is not the answer. Neither are surveys, or focus groups, or any other kind of data for that matter, regardless of how much of it you have.

Robert Rose, a senior analyst with the Digital Clarity Group, believes that we have reached a critical point where marketers must recognize that all data is embedded as part of a bigger context. More importantly, Rose believes that while people have been talking for years about delivering contextual analytics to allow for a continuous, integrated process that builds upon each dataset, the time has arrived where it *must* happen before we can bring meaning to the staggering amount of information now available.

This is a fundamental tenet of contextual analytics. It requires that market researchers accept and acknowledge that no single dataset by itself will ever provide sufficient context to make fully informed decisions. The mission then is to identify all of the various data sources that are relevant, and then link those datasets so that they can work together.

So ... how exactly do we do that?

PART II

THE FUNDAMENTALS OF CONTEXTUAL ANALYTICS

Market research is about making money.

The contextual analytics model I present over the next three chapters is not intended to be appropriate for scientific research, psychology surveys, or other academic endeavors. The pursuit of knowledge is a noble one, but in the business world we have to temper it with the pursuit of profit (and vice versa). I want to help my clients make as much money as they can, as efficiently and cost-effectively as possible.

Fortunately, that's what contextual analytics is best at.

THE FOUR ELEMENTS OF MARKET RESEARCH

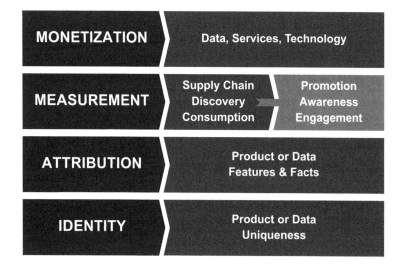

5

DATA SOURCES

*Knowledge has become the key economic resource
and the dominant, if not the only,
source of competitive advantage.*

—PETER DRUCKER

In the Visa versus Vons scenario, you could have either breadth or depth.

In true contextual analyses, you must have both.

No matter how powerful of a microscope you use, one piece of the puzzle can only reveal so much. But haphazardly putting together different puzzle pieces does not seem like much of a strategy, does it? When pursuing contextual analytics, we need to know the sources of our data and to be aware of the gaps. What's more, we have to be intentional about how and where we gather the pieces to fill in those gaps.

There are three primary types of market research data: measurement, identity, and attribution. Measurement data comes from primary data (such as surveys and focus groups) or secondary data (preexisting research or databases). Attribution data contains the characteristics or features of a product or dataset so that richer insights can be obtained. Identity data contains the unique properties that let you know that two different datasets are about the exact same thing.

Each of the three deserves its own detailed attention. Since measurement data comprises the vast majority of data available today, and is where most companies make their money, we will start there. But since it encompasses so much, we need to further break measurement data down into three distinct categories:

1. Supply chain data

2. Consumption chain data

3. Discovery loop data

Each represents a different phase of the product's lifecycle. As such, in order to perform an effective contextual analysis, you must have data from each of these three categories before you can fully understand the story behind a product.

The Supply Chain

The Supply Chain Management Council defines its domain as "all activities involved in sourcing and procurement, conversion, and all logistics management activities. It includes coordination and collaboration with channel partners, which can be suppliers, intermediaries, third-party service providers, and customers."

From a measurement perspective, supply chain data represents all data associated with the product from a tangible perspective (other than actual consumption of the product). Practically speaking, supply chain data answers such questions as:

- "How much did it cost to make the product?"

- "How many units of the product are in the warehouse?"

- "How many units of the product have we sold?"

- "How are we transporting the product or its raw materials?"
- "What regulatory or compliance fees were paid to legally sell the product?"

You may notice that supply chain data is, by its nature, relatively linear. From a tracking perspective, it starts at the origin of cost of goods and ends at the consumer purchase point. It may also include secondary sales activities, such as trade-ins, used product sales, or the recycling process.

THE CONSUMPTION CHAIN

The supply chain offers a rich set of data points. The design and manufacture of a product or service involves a host of activities (à la "the billion dollar paperclip"). But even though the supply chain may offer a host of data, it all comes from the basic perspective of production and distribution. It reveals nothing about how the end customer uses it. Since everyone consumes products differently, just one dataset from the consumption chain (also referred to as "telemetry data", "user-activity data", or "macine-data") can offer multimillion-dollar insights into how the consumer market may be segmented.

Take a person at a gas station buying Dr. Pepper. They may buy one Dr. Pepper from the cooler for the road and at the same time buy a six-pack for the weekend. Dr. Pepper's manufacturer and every other beverage company packages, distributes, and sells the exact same product at least two different ways for the same consumer—because of the different ways that one person consumes their products.

The point-of-sale (POS) data from the supply chain should deliver all the information needed about when, where, and how a purchaser acquires the product from the supplier or retailer. But POS data does not provide many—if any—insights into how the individual actually consumes the product.

Did they sit down and guzzle the entire can right there at the gas station? Did they share the six-pack with their friends, or drink them over an extended period on their road trip? Did they hold the can with their left hand or their right? Did they pour the can into a glass? Did they mix the soda with alcohol?

One of the most famous uses of consumption data was in 1987 when Bob Crandall, then-CEO of American Airlines, cut one olive from first-class salads to save $40,000 a year—a savings of about a million dollars over time. Crandall's research indicated that the consumption experience—and by extension, overall consumer satisfaction—would not be affected by the change. He was right. Even though the airlines may still operate in the red, it's not because passengers are mad about one less olive in their salads.

Another airline CEO decided to push the findings of consumption data to the limit. In 2010, Michael O'Leary at Ryanair proposed allowing passengers a lower airfare but requiring them to stand for the whole flight. (Not to mention a surcharge for nearly everything else, including $2 per bathroom trip.) Even though the proposal was shot down within a matter of days by the European Aviation Safety Agency, O'Leary made a plausible case. He argued that the majority of passengers do very little during their flights other than listen to music, read a magazine, or sleep. The collected consumption data indicated that for short flights, passengers would much rather pay less than have additional amenities that they would wind up ignoring anyway.

O'Leary's proposal was radical, but that is the point: the data that can point to new innovation, and opportunities often exists beyond the supply chain. Without fully understanding how customers consume your products, you cannot understand what factors may or may not influence their decisions to buy.

Smart companies should want to know why consumers act the way they do in relation to their offerings. Advertisers are keenly interested not just in what percentage of people see their promotion, but also where they were when they saw it, and under what circumstances. Did they see the television spot during its original allotted run time? Or was it at a later date as a result of recording a show? Did they change the channel while the advertisement was running? What other channels were they switching between when they saw the ad?

Regardless of the method or medium of collection, consumption data aims to answer questions like:

- "How many people watch television on big screens vs. small screens?"

- "What was the temperature outside when a customer purchased a soda?"

- "How aggressively do drivers accelerate when the traffic signal turns green?"

- "How many customers read the nutritional information before purchasing their frozen dinner?"

In many cases, consumption data has replaced traditional quantitative or qualitative surveys. (After all, consumers' actions speak louder than their words, right?) Former Google executive and current

Yahoo! CEO Marissa Mayer provided an interesting example during a presentation at the Web 2.0 conference in 2011. She outlined how Google took a survey of users and asked them how they would improve search results. The survey takers responded that they would like more results on the page. So, Google increased the number of search results on one page. Consequently, traffic and revenue dropped by over 20%. Knowing Google is a multibillion-dollar company, you can imagine how much of a loss that represented.

Why did traffic drop so precipitously? As a result of more results displayed, the page load time rose from 0.4 seconds to 0.9 seconds. That literal half-second delay negatively impacted the consumption experience. Had Google not been monitoring the load time, they would never have been able to connect the dots, resulting in an eventual loss of billions of dollars over time.

The power of consumption data is clear, but a little knowledge can be a dangerous thing. Consider the earlier example of Zynga, with their development services based almost solely on consumption data, as a counterexample. Obviously, companies need a broader understanding of the consumer beyond the actual consumption of a product or service.

That brings us to the third place to find measurement data: the discovery loop.

THE DISCOVERY LOOP

The year was 1989. In a remote area of Iowa, farmer Ray Kinsella woke up one morning, mowed down his corn, and built a baseball field. The catalyst was the one sentence he heard in his head: "If you build it, they will come."

Kevin Costner's *Field of Dreams* captured our imaginations, grossed over $100 million, and was nominated for three Academy Awards. Unfortunately for most companies, "if you build it, they will buy" just doesn't work. Potential consumers need to be aware that something exists before they can purchase it. That is, they need to discover it first.

In contextual analytics, the measurement data related to this process of awareness is referred to as the discovery loop. Unlike supply and consumption data that largely operate as linear experiences, the ecosystem around product discovery is often circuitous and evolving. A consumer's perception of a product is always changing: what they hear about it, what they share about it, and their experiences gained from consuming it. As such, the discovery loop is perhaps the most complex type of measurement data. Because of this complexity, before we can examine it we need to break it down into its three subcomponents: promotional data, awareness data, and engagement data.

Promotional data is generally the most obtainable data, centering primarily on a product's visibility among its potential consumers, usually related to how much was spent on media marketing. The types of questions promotional data answers include:

- "How many advertisements were run?"
- "What mix of direct media was used to promote the product?"
- "How many articles were written about the product?"
- "How many editorial assets were deployed?"
- "What type of advertising was done inside the retail store?"
- "How many newspaper inserts or circulars were distributed?"

Awareness data, on the other hand, measures how many consumers became aware of the product and, based on that awareness, what their perceptions were. Unlike almost every other area of measurement data, awareness data represents not only objective and/or numerical measurements, but also quantitative and qualitative measures that provide insights into the consumer's motivation. Because of this, awareness data is impacted not just by what consumers learn through the promotional efforts of product suppliers, but also through how consumers interact with the product on their own. Awareness data answers questions such as:

- "How many people are aware my product exists?"
- "How did people hear about my product?"
- "Where did people learn about my product?"
- "Do people perceive the product as good or bad?"
- "What do people think of the previous products released by the company?"
- "How is the product thought of compared to its competitors?"

The final aspect of measurement data within the discovery loop is engagement. **Engagement data** differs from awareness data, although the two data sets are often mistaken for one another. Whereas awareness data measures overall knowledge and perception of the product, engagement data measures how a consumer has interacted with a product outside of the supply chain or consumption chain. Questions that engagement data answers include:

- "How many people visited the website for the product?"

- "How many people watched the video trailer for the product?"

- "How many people have posted about the product through social media?"

- "How many people have discussed the product in online forums?"

The discovery loop is where the majority of the market researcher's world resides. Promotional data provides insight into what messages about the product were created and how they were distributed; Awareness data offers information on how successful the efforts of improving consumer perception and awareness of the product were and: Engagement data sheds light on how effective the promotional and awareness efforts have been.

THE NEED FOR DIFFERENT TYPES OF DATA

After reviewing all the various types of data that compose a product's story, you may find it disheartening to realize how little your company captures of the total picture.

Knowing how many times a web surfer visits a website before finally buying something is a good fact—but if you do not know why they did it or how they consumed your product, you still have only a tiny piece of a very big puzzle.

The data that represents the supply chain, consumption chain, and discovery loop exists in a variety of forms, coming from both data resellers and internal collection. This variety is essential to contextual analytics. However, it is much more than simply making sure your data comes from more than one place. It is about intentionally selecting each source according to the aspect of the product story you need represented and the types of insights it can provide.

But more than that, you must also be cognizant of the quality of each dataset you introduce into your contextual analysis ecosystem.

6

DATA QUALITY

To write it took three months; to conceive it—three minutes;
to collect the data in it—all my life.
—F. Scott Fitzgerald on writing *This Side of Paradise*

"Garbage in, garbage out," right?

Every researcher and decision-maker knows the saying and tries to abide by it when collecting and analyzing data. But it takes on a new twist with contextual analytics. Perhaps the more relevant saying is, "A chain is only as strong as its weakest link." As you establish a contextual framework, you are laying the structure for a strong and vibrant data ecosystem. But you can pollute your entire ecosystem with just one low quality dataset.

It is critically important to understand that not all data is created equally and appreciate the varying levels. In this regard, data can be placed into three broad categories, determined (in part) by the method of collection: captured, observed, or sampled.

CAPTURED DATA

"Captured data" sits on the highest rung of the ladder of quality.

It is collected in real time as an event happens and, by necessity, is almost always digital in nature. The links people go to after a Google search, the real-time stream of what a TV watcher sees, the average delay time for a particular flight, FedEx's shipment tracking, a factory line's output—companies track, capture, and store data like this automatically, all the time, every time. The dataset represents 100% of the monitored activities.

Right now, captured data is on the verge of explosive growth. In their first paper describing the "Internet of Everything," IT company Cisco explained that many organizations are currently experiencing the "internet of things"; that is, the networked connection of physical objects such as PCs, tablets, and smartphones. As "things" add capabilities like context awareness, increased processing power, and energy independence—and as more people and more new types of information are connected—the internet of things will become the Internet of Everything: a network of networks, containing billions or even trillions of data nodes, connecting people in more relevant and valuable ways than ever before.

For example, EEDAR is exploring a system that connects sensors embedded in a person's clothing to video games and medical databases. The system collects user activity from the embedded sensors, such as exercise or gameplay. By integrating that data with a linked medical dataset (based on exercise information and their physician's recommendations), the player can be challenged with in-game exercises suited to their unique needs. Plus, the player can share the data with their doctor so they can monitor their health, or even send the information to their insurance company in exchange for a lower premium.

But something like this can only happen via the high quality of captured data.

OBSERVED DATA

One rung lower sits "observed data." With this type, a researcher attempts to collect 100% of a particular dataset with minimal bias, just like with captured data. However, because observed data is almost always collected by an external process (either manually or through some level of automation), its quality is necessarily lower.

For instance, imagine a high school kid standing at the entrance to the zoo with a hand tally, counting everyone who comes into the park. While he may come close to 100% accuracy, his count will always have some degree of questionability. Was he trained properly? Does he know he should count babies in strollers or carriers? Does he know to look for the reentry stamp on people coming back into the park? Observed data presents opportunities for human error not present in captured data. Additionally, as an external process, there may be certain elements of the data that cannot be observed.

In *Reliability, Maintainability and Risk*, Dr. David Smith, former chairman of the Safety and Reliability Society, cited a number of studies documenting errors across a variety of human tasks. His results found that an average of five out of every one hundred calculator entries are incorrect when entering ten digits or more, and that 3% of people incorrectly read low resolution text when managing data entry. If these types of rates are accurate, when combined with the volume of information being created today, this certainly brings the reliability of observed data into question.

But while observed data is not as good as captured data, it is better than the third alternative.

Sampled Data

Sample data sits on the bottom rung of the quality ladder. It inherently reflects that it is not always cost effective (or even possible) to capture 100% of a potential dataset. As such, researchers resort to sampled data to represent the whole dataset. Despite that, this is a case where "something is better than nothing."

The essential key in utilizing any kind of data, especially sampled data, is to appreciate the nuances of the sample and survey methodology, and to then proceed accordingly. The major difference between the quality and reliability of most sampled measurement data is:

- the quality of the survey respondents, focus group, panel, etc.

- the methodology used to extract the data from the sample

- the structure and format of the questions used within the extraction process

By definition, surveys are information collected from a sample of qualified candidates, i.e., people's opinions. But just how representative of a sample—which is to say how relevant—are the respondents? As soon as an analyst begins to make judgment calls about who should or should not be included in the questionnaire, they introduce bias into the data. Should they include only Pepsi drinkers? Are non-Pepsi drinkers relevant? For that matter, are non-cola drinkers relevant?

Right behind these important questions comes another one: how biased will the method of collection be? If presidential pollsters had known to ask this crucial question, we would never have had the famous photograph of president-elect Harry S. Truman holding a newspaper with the headline "DEWEY DEFEATS TRUMAN." The newspapers went to press predicting a win for Republican candidate Thomas E. Dewey based on phone surveys. In 1948, however, telephones were found more in the homes of the wealthy, and these people tended to vote Republican. Essentially, the research project asked representatives of wealthy homeowners who they were most likely to vote for instead of asking a sample of the general voting populace.

In spite of correcting for these errors in today's research, this same sampling bias still occurs. A perfect modern example is the federal "do not call list" (DNCL) that prevents telemarketers and market researchers, among others, from calling households who opt into the list. One study from UC Berkeley examined the demographics and found that the DNCL skews white, with higher incomes and education. Therefore, some studies that rely on phone surveys are already biased against wealthier, more educated whites simply because of the particular method of data collection.

In the vast majority of cases, when a company hires a firm to conduct survey-based market research, the respondents are purchased through wholesalers known as "panel providers." Very few market research companies maintain their own personal panels. Those who do are generally specialized around a particular type of respondent that may be difficult to reach through wholesalers. For many survey-based research initiatives, it is not uncommon for multiple wholesalers to be used to help achieve the quota requirements for the assignment. The issue with the online panel providers is that in many cases people have had to "sign up" to be a participant of the panel. By its nature, that means there are portions of any audience that will never be represented in these panels because they are not ever going to sign up in the first place!

Researchers became aware of sample biases in phone surveys with the 1948 election, but this is not the only place they encounter such issues. Online surveys come with their own set of problems, too. Believe it or not, there are people whose day job is taking online surveys all day. If they can take a survey for two dollars and do five surveys per hour, they can make more than minimum wage from the comfort of their own home! The real pros in this charade can make as much as fifteen or even twenty dollars an hour, gaming the system hour after hour. They know how to delete the cookies in their browser or how to mimic the actions of genuine respondents to pass all the built-in checks and balances. Of course they don't care about the accuracy of the information they provide; their only concern is finishing as quickly as possible and getting paid. In some cases, these disingenuous survey-takers comprise as much as 20-40% of an online sample. It's a very real concern: in the 2013 Greenbook Research Industry Trends Report, over 50% of suppliers and 40% of clients expressed a belief that the quality of online samples is worse than commonly acknowledged in the trade.

Even if you do get a full sample of clean target respondents, there are other challenges that plague survey-based research. For one, the composition of a survey affects how accurate their answers are. If the survey is too long, too complex, too wordy, too boring, or too much of anything else, the survey-taker may stop caring toward the end and just click random answers to hurry up so they can go for another cup of coffee.

In the past, statisticians responded to such discrepancies by saying that enough survey data would correct for these minuscule errors. Essentially, they said, "It's fine." But today, "fine" or "good enough" is not good enough. The reality has changed, but the methods have not kept pace.

In an ever-increasing connection of data, one bad dataset can call the entire ecosystem into question.

Managing With Different Quality Datasets

You could use any of these methods to collect data on the same aspect of a product, but all three methods will yield different results. The good news is contextual analytics does a better job of managing the risk associated with varied collection methodologies than any other form of research.

Let's say that BMW wants to collect data on the satisfaction of new car purchasers at different dealerships. They have a number of ways to collect this information. The delivery agent may ask the new driver to fill out a small survey before they hand over the keys. The same driver may also receive a phone or email survey a few weeks afterwards from an independent company. (Of course, when the salesperson hands over the keys at the dealership, they inevitably say, "Look, when they call you to rate your experience, make sure you give me all fives, okay?" Talk about biasing the dataset!). They may even look at data in terms of how many people who trade-in a BMW purchase another one versus those who leave the brand altogether.

To examine the varying results from those analyzing those different datasets, BMW would need to collect additional metadata. Data points that the researchers could include might be the time of day the surveys were completed (people may be more willing to rate things well fresh in the morning versus late at night), where the respondents were contacted (they may be less willing to give open answers in a work environment than at their home), and how close together the surveys were conducted (the "new car" feeling may have worn off after so many weeks), or the economic conditions when the car was traded in (people may have been forced to buy cheaper cars in hard economic times).

This is where contextual analytics truly shines. Whether captured, observed or sampled, a contextual framework forces these datasets to work in harmony with one another. Each element of information can fill gaps where possible and validate or dispute findings where there is overlap. In other words, every additional dataset yields additional context that enhances the researchers' understanding of the whole picture.

Of course, achieving this harmony requires that there be a way to get these disparate datasets to work together in the first place. That is, you have to connect the dots.

7

DATA LINKS

*Only if every user has a common and exact understanding
of the data can it be exchanged trouble-free.*
—ISO/IEC 11179 Metadata Registry Specification

In order to see the overlap between various datasets you must first be able to connect the data points that are common to both. Without the ability to find these intersections, you just have data floating around in space, isolated and dramatically underutilized.

Creating the data necessary to link disparate datasets across industries and fields of study isn't an easy task, but the rewards for doing so are immense.

Imagine if, say, all psychologists could agree on common attribute fields in their research. From around the world, they could perform studies in their own clinics and population groups, and then upload everything to a global master database, thereby exponentially increasing the value and context of all the data residing there. Imagine the possibilities if every single psychologist had access to their peers' data. Say one psychologist studied the reasons behind criminals getting rearrested but another studied arrested protestors, such as those of

Occupy Wall Street. If both their datasets had the same fields (with the exact same parameters, definitions, etc.) they could instantly multiply the depth and/or breadth of their research. The first psychologist could glean a much richer insight from understanding a narrow category while the second could compare a specific study group against a far broader population.

The challenge centers on making sure that their data fields and categories are—I mean *absolutely*—the same. Take ethnicity. Both of our psychologists would have to define it exactly the same for any kind of proper analysis to work. If one psychologist makes a distinction between Koreans and Thais but another one simply lumps all these two groups together as Asian/Pacific Islander, neither one can use the other's data without redefining everything.

With such things as ethnicity or religion, everyone understands that a high degree of subjectivity comes into play. But tangible manufactured products and features should fall into specific slots and categories easily. Right?

If only it were that easy!

SAME PRODUCT, DIFFERENT IDENTITIES

Regardless of the classification system any company or industry association creates, there are always businesses, organizations, and experts who disagree. Even well-established classification systems like Universal Product Codes (UPCs) have their flaws. In principle, they seem like a great way to track a product. Each product variation has its own UPC so retailers can digitally keep track of inventory and sales.

You might not realize it, but even those product identifiers you see as barcodes on the back of most products are not "universal." In other markets, the same product may have a European Article Number, Canadian Article Number, Amazon Standard Identification Number, Japanese Article Number, or Global Trade Item Number. At EEDAR, there is a team responsible for the unenviable task of maintaining a database just to keep track of all the ways different retailers and countries refer to the exact same thing. (In the database world, this would be referred to as a "primary key.")

I mean, wouldn't it be helpful if everyone could just call the same thing by the same name?

Unfortunately, that is still a pipe dream.

One day, if Cisco's prediction for the Internet of Everything is realized, all forms of data may be able to communicate with each other…but we are many years from that day. In today's world, we must live with the ugly truth that the vast majority of measurement data produced just does not play well together.

Say I wanted to do a research project on one of my favorite products: whiskey. I could go into any retailer and find the UPC on the bottle; hypothetically, let's say it is 1-23456-78912-3. But if I went to the distillery and asked for the statistics on product 1-23456-78912-3 the head distiller would probably have no idea what I meant. After showing him the bottle, he might say something like, "Oh, you mean the eighteen-year-old sherry cask batch from 1992? Why didn't you say so in the first place? I can give you all the information you want!"

If I called the public relations firm to ask about product 1-23456-78912-3 and/or "the eighteen-year-old sherry cask batch from 1992," they would have no idea what I was talking about. Of course, after I show them the bottle they might say, "Oh, the Limited Release Highland Park? Why didn't you just say so?!"

This is the exact situation I have faced many times over my career in working with analytics. The retailer, manufacturer, and marketer of the exact same product cannot even agree on a unique identifier for a product they all handle, much less create a compatible system that reads data as the product goes from the source to the consumer.

This is the primary role of identity in contextual analytics. At the identity layer, each dataset's dedicated identity field is put into its appropriate place according to the type of data it is.

THE SAME STORY FOR THE ATTRIBUTION LAYER

The identity field is really just a unique attribute of any product—albeit the crucial one, since without a common identifier, no two datasets can work together. Just as companies cannot agree on how to identify the same product, they cannot agree on how identify the different features and attributes of the product.

The data crunchers of the world could revolutionize nearly every field of human endeavor—if only we could get data that should work together to actually do it! The reason this is such an arduous task is because it is such a complicated one. When you create the attribute fields for a product, you have to take into account all the factors surrounding it, such as the abstraction of the data.

Take for example geographic identity. If one dataset tracks data at the county level, another at the state level, and another at the national level, how do you account for that? You cannot assign everything to the county because that would require you to guess on how to break up the data tracked at the state and national levels. You could use the national level as the least common denominator and "roll-up" all the county- and state-level attributes, but then you lose granularity from certain datasets.

It's a dilemma!

Through my experience with attribution in the contextual analytics systems I have developed, the answer is: you do them all! You create systems that allow you to say which counties are in which states, and which states are in which countries. You also develop different rules that allow you to experiment with breaking down aggregate data when required. Of course, this is less accurate, so you have to account for potential errors in the data created when you do so. But until all data is consistently created at the same granularity across the board, it is simply something that has to be done.

In some cases, datasets cannot be linked by a unique identifier and so, by necessity, must be linked via an attribution field. Take for example a perfume company. One dataset may contain all the ingredients of every perfume: rose oil, lavender oil, purified water, etc. Another dataset may have the cost of various types of rose oil over time. In this instance, it would be necessary to join the datasets on the specific type of rose oil used for that perfume.

But just as you have to consider the overall quality of a dataset by its method of collection, you must consider the quality of specific attribution data by its method of collection.

ATTRIBUTION DATA: CURATED VS. CROWD-SOURCED

The overarching goal in contextual analytics is to obtain as much attribution data about any data source used as possible. That means *every* data source. It isn't always about the demographics of people, or the color of the packaging. It can be just as critical to know how many stores participated in submitting their data for a sales estimate, or how many different television channels were monitored to estimate advertising volumes. The more these attributes can be identified, normalized and then consistently tracked across the disparate sources within an attribution layer, the more effective your contextual analytics approach can identify external influencing factors on the generated information.

Now when it comes to attribution data, I know of only two ways to create it: curate it by hand, or collect it via automated systems. That is, either build the tools, taxonomies, and systems to collect it internally; or leverage technology and the masses to populate the information (i.e., crowdsource it). Hand curated metadata takes a lot of time and, therefore, a lot of money. Small wonder then that ever since *The Wisdom of Crowds* was authored by James Surowiecki, many companies have chosen to leverage the power of the internet in an attempt to let the market create this data for them.

This can work quite well in some cases. Take Google for example. The algorithms they have developed take often unrelated words and quickly provide accurate results when users search on the internet. The brilliance of Google's search system is how it learns what is and is not relevant: it does so organically. In other words, by crowdsourcing.

When someone types in a search term, Google lists potential

matches in order of how relevant the page probably is to the user. The more the search giant refines its algorithm, the better it gets at giving us exactly what we want. To determine part of the formula for how relevant a page is likely to be, Google tracks users' actions. If a user goes through a string of results before finally clicking on a page, Google assumes that the previous search strings were not the most relevant answer. It adjusts the weight of the results for the search terms based on the site the user finally clicked on. When a different user uses one of those search terms in the future, Google then presents what it guesses is the more relevant result. Track what enough people do, the logic says, and we can determine what most people are looking for.

Apple—Google's competition in many aspects—offers iTunes, which is powered, in part, by Gracenote, a company that sells metadata on media products. When someone puts a music CD into their computer, Gracenote can return album name, artist(s), cover art, and genre. But the person may decide that Gracenote classified their CD wrong; instead of R&B, the music listener decides it should be classified as Latino Pop. Gracenote records the change. If enough people do that, Gracenote may decide that the album should be classified as Latino Pop since so many other people seem to think so.

Here's a hypothetical dilemma: what if 50.1% of users call it Latino Pop and 49.9% say it's R&B? Who wins? If the majority rules, then 49.9% of the potential market may not find the album because they would not think to search under Latino Pop for emerging artists they're interested in. Should some people's vote have more weight than others? Should it be classified under both genres?

On the flip side, consider *The Dana Owens Album* by rapper Queen Latifah. She made her mark in hip hop and R&B, but this particular album is a compilation of mostly jazz, with songs like "I Put a Spell on You" or "California Dreamin'." Yet in iTunes you will find it under R&B/Soul because that is where the rest of her albums are. In this instance, crowdsourcing has failed; "the people" have not helped Gracenote identify that this is primarily a jazz album and should not be anywhere near the R&B section. Plenty of classic jazz enthusiasts would love the album—if only they knew about it. But you will not find them perusing the R&B category.

All this is not to say that there is not a place for crowdsourced data, because there is. This is simply my counterargument to the movement spawned by *Wisdom of Crowds* that essentially said, "Ask enough people and the truth will emerge."

Bollocks.

Managing "Good Enough" Data

As in all things with data, there are pros and cons.

Crowdsourced attribution is a viable option for some types of attribution collection under carefully scrutinized conditions. It is usually good enough to get us in the ballpark of the real answer. Perhaps Gracenote ran the numbers and decided that paying an identity company to curate the data would not result in enough sales to justify the costs. Yeah, some jazz listeners might not find *The Dana Owens Album*, but how many jazz fans are there? Would the error in classification disrupt their revenue stream? Perhaps not sufficiently enough to pay someone to re-categorize the album.

Of course someone purchasing the data from Gracenote to use for a different purpose may disagree. If the data was to be used within contextual analysis focused on financial planning, such inaccuracies could have dire consequences. So it is important to know a few things when one is using crowdsourced attribution data. How do the crowdsourcing rules work? Where do the samples reside? How are conflicts that emerge resolved? When there is a 51/49 split, does it refer the data up to a specialist to make a hand-curated determination instead of a computerized one? What rules and training are in place to ensure that is done consistently? Crowdsourcing is not always a bad thing. Sometimes, good enough is all that is needed. You just need to know what strings come attached.

On the opposite end of the spectrum is the brute force option: companies creating their own internal attribution datasets. Utilizing their industry expertise, and available best practices, they could hire a staff of internal researchers to do this specific task. For some companies, this is absolutely the best option. For others, the cost of this effort may be prohibitive vis-à-vis the output.

The middle ground between the two extremes is outsourcing to a specialist company for curated identity and attribution data that can be leveraged into their contextual analytics framework. There is good reason for exploring this option. As market research flourishes under contextual analysis, vendor relevance is shifting away from mammoth companies who try to sell data to every possible vertical. In their place sit smaller, more agile companies specializing in market niches, creating highly accurate attribution information, and aggregating data relevant to the specific needs of that industry.

All of this may come as a bit of a shock to the multimillion-dollar research and consulting firms operating under decades old systems today. But this is not the first time a revolution based on data has changed the game.

Moneyball, by Michael Lewis, retold the story of Billy Beane and his disruptive contribution to the game of baseball. In 2002, Beane amazingly took the Oakland Athletics to the World Series on a relative shoestring budget of only $41 million (compared to the Yankees' $125 million). However, the disruptive approach he used in getting there was both heralded and ridiculed by the entrenched baseball community: doing away with scouts and gut-based decisions, and embracing a data-driven approach to optimizing player selection and team placement. In the book, Lewis cites John Henry, owner of the Boston Red Sox, giving his view on the impact Beane's data-driven methods had on the game:

> *You've taken it in the teeth out there, but the first guy through the wall, it always gets bloody, always. It's the threat of not just the way of doing business, but in their minds it's threatening the game. It's threatening their livelihoods. It's threatening their jobs. It's threatening the way that they do things. And every time that happens, whether it's the government, or a way of doing business, whatever it is, the people that are holding the reins...they go bat shit crazy. But anybody who is not building a team right now, and building it using your model, they're dinosaurs. They'll be sitting on their ass on the sofa in October, watching the Boston Red Sox win the World Series.*

It didn't happen that October...but the next year the Boston Red Sox did win the World Series, breaking an eighty-six-year drought and forever changing the game.

PART III

THE BUSINESS OF CONTEXTUAL ANALYTICS

In the Age of Analytics, manufacturing and distribution costs will be augmented with new metrics—the costs of know, the flow of know, and the costs of not-knowing. The information value chain —arguably a huge potential source of competitive advantage— is undocumented and unmanaged in most enterprises today.

—THORNTON MAY, *THE NEW KNOW: INNOVATION POWERED BY ANALYTICS*

So at this point we know that:

1. Measurement data exists in three areas: the supply chain, the consumption chain, and the discovery loop (comprising promotion, awareness, and engagement).

2. The quality of measurement data depends on whether it is captured, observed, or sampled.

3. A dataset's full potential will go unrealized until the identity and attribution layers exist that allow each dataset to link to all the others.

These are the fundamentals of creating insights that unlock the story behind the product; they see the whole picture instead of isolated events.

However, to become adept at navigating the world of market research, you need to understand the three core ways vendors monetize data, as well as the differing perspectives of each player in the relationship: vendor, client, and consumer.

If you sell products that interact with contextual analytics, then you should understand what is driving your clients as they become more discriminating with their research budgets. If you are a data buyer, you should be aware of the new options you have for creating your own data systems. If you are a consumer, you should be exploring how far you can push your lines of inquiry.

As such, Part III focuses on the business of contextual analytics.

8

THE EVOLUTION IS AT HAND

*Analytics is the ability to…draw from all kinds
of information and turn it into a story.*
—FRANK WRENN, MARKET RESEARCH MANAGER
AT DELTA AIRLINES

"Contextual analytics sounds so promising…why haven't we done this before?"

A number of factors have prevented contextual analysis in the past. While it has always been a theoretical possibility, relatively recent technological advances in the data vendor world have made it a commercial possibility. The main problem has centered on the vast amount of data it takes to perform a decent contextual analysis. As such, Big Data was a necessary precursor.

As we discussed, a contextual approach requires a breadth of data sources (i.e. variety) as well as a sufficient depth of information (i.e. volume) to enhance other datasets. One of the first obstacles was the lack of computers advanced enough to collect the sheer amount of data. Even after the advent of such, most companies had to wait until the computers were also affordable. As such, the systems needed to practically amass sufficient data have only been around for about two decades.

Then, too, companies faced the problem of storing so much data. Today, the price of servers and even cloud servers has dramatically diminished. But even after those factors fell into place, businesses faced the bottleneck of transmitting the massive amounts of data they had stored. Unless they had on-site data analysts, they faced enormous financial and logistical challenges to get their data into the hands of third-party companies. In short, the entire technical infrastructure simply did not exist.

Until now.

Today, such collection, storage, and transmission of previously unimaginable amounts of data have become commercially practical. Most data-centric companies have the resources, people, and technology to collect as much data as they want and send it anywhere in the world. Previously insurmountable technology challenges are now mere footnotes in market research initiatives.

Unfortunately, plenty of market research companies still have their head stuck in the sand, doing business like they did in the 90s (or 80s…or 70s…). Traditionally, the market research industry has been dominated by a few key types of measurement data. Whether TV ratings, sell-through data, or survey information, it is now clear that the multimillion-dollar behemoths who once dominated this space are now faced with challenging times. While these data providers still supply an important service, the needs of the industries they serve have evolved beyond the core capabilities of these giants.

Instead of being limited to data from one or two sampled sources in the supply chain, you can demand captured data from throughout the product lifecycle. The power of a "brand" is no longer a soft science; marketers can collect hard numbers to understand how it affects consumers' adoption of products (via the discovery loop). Clickstream data captured via a person's cable TV box can now be aligned with social media data to discover exactly when people abandoned a new pilot and *why*.

But there is a downside for some in the ecosystem of market research, too. As data becomes more abundant, it becomes more of a commodity. Today, even tiny startup companies can compete on providing data. In many cases, they have completely disrupted "untouchable" market segments held by the incumbent giants.

DATA-AS-A-SERVICE

Over the last decade Salesforce has quickly risen to be one of the most adopted technologies in client relationship management. It achieved this by delivering a completely new experience in the form of software-as-a-service (SaaS), delivering their offerings via the internet with no installation required and virtually no computer hardware limitations.

The truth is that SaaS has been around in various forms since as far back as the 1960s. IBM offered utility computing (somewhat akin to today's Amazon Web Services) to banks way back before the internet was really even understood. But it was not until the internet revolution of the 90s that the world was ready to embrace "the future," as sold by the market's heavyweights: Google Apps, Office365, Adobe Creative

Cloud, Apple iCloud, and more. Today, nearly every new software product is designed with some aspect of SaaS in mind.

What you may not know is that the research industry has also had a similar disruption with the supply of data. Data-as-a-Service (DaaS) is dramatically changing the cost structures and pricing models of measurement, attribution, and identity data. Hoovers, a subsidiary of the renowned Dun & Bradstreet, now supplies real-time data on millions of businesses via an interface. Of course, they charge thousands of dollars a year for this information, despite much of it relying on crowdsourced data, with the participating companies updating their own information via their Dun & Bradstreet profiles.

On the other hand, Factual.com provides a similar service that allows up to 10,000 retrievals per day at no cost at all. You could have a savvy engineer in your IT department set up an account and be retrieving data from their service before you finish reading this book! Of course, if you want to capture some kind of specific datasets, there are companies like PromptCloud and Mozenda who can customize web-scrapers to pull all kinds of data from online sources into custom databases. Just remember to check with your lawyers about what you plan to grab!

DATA: COMMODITIZED AND OPEN SOURCED

By definition, a commodity has smaller profit margins. In the business of data, we are now witnessing a race to the bottom: smaller companies with lower overhead offering the good-enough data I have been talking about. Despite the loss of quality, some of these companies are displacing long-time market leaders in many segments. What does it mean for the market research industry? Individual commodity suppliers are losing their leverage. It is not the death knell for those pure data providers—but the stakes are rising, not just in data, but in technology and services as well.

One of my first startups was an online magazine back in 1999. In the midst of the dot-com boom, I had to purchase my first server cluster and pay for a dedicated hosting connection. I paid a staggering $170 per megabit for internet access; my computers were $7,000 each and less powerful than many of today's smartphones. To host my 30-megabits-per-month site cost me $5,100 a month in bandwidth.

My, how times have changed!

Just a few months ago I set up a new datacenter at $4.75 a megabit; that is, at less than 3% of what I paid back then. With such substantially lower costs for internet bandwidth and infrastructure, one of the significant barriers to entry has fallen away. It has never been cheaper to work with data.

Beyond hardware and infrastructure another major disruptor in the world of market research has come to the fore: Open Source. The Open Source movement is backed by programmers throughout the world working together to create systems that are virtually all free. Couple that with low-cost bandwidth and hardware, and you have a mixture for a major market shift.

THE NEW GAME OF MARKET RESEARCH

The competition this fosters will ultimately prove to be a good thing for the end-consumers of information. But with profit migrating away from the suppliers of measurement data to those companies able to unlock the story hidden behind it all, the behemoths will be forced to transition with the market if they want to survive.

Every rule of the data game has changed and continues to change. Data, in all forms, is now more readily available than ever before, and will only continue to become cheaper and more accessible. The cost and availability of technology systems, from storage to transmission, are also at all-time lows. They, too, will only get cheaper and more powerful as we move forward.

All of this provides an advantageous environment for contextual analytics. By providing a clear blueprint for how these various data and technology systems can be brought together and leveraging the emerging data tiers of attribution and identity, an entire new segment has arisen: the insights provider industry.

As I said, the rules of the game have changed. It is no longer enough to be a purveyor of data. Your customers can buy cheaper data elsewhere (even if it is not as good as yours). They can buy the technology platforms and the systems to analyze the data themselves. Everything that can be turned into a commodity has been (or shortly will be).

I quoted Peter Drucker saying that knowledge is the only remaining competitive advantage. The bottom line is that if you want to stay in the business of data, you must embrace some aspect of contextual analytics so that you can provide unique value. Clearly, I do not think every company should rush out and become the full-service contextual analytics provider in their respective industry (although I hope many consider it).

I am simply advocating that you recognize the necessity for moving to an insights-based role within the evolving ecosystem of market research. As contextual analytics continues to unlock billions of dollars in the data companies already have (not to mention the additional data being collected every day), it will soon be the dominant framework in our business.

Does your company have a plan for how you will adapt?

9

HOW TO MAKE MONEY IN MARKET RESEARCH

If you don't have a competitive advantage, don't compete!
—Jack Welch, former CEO of GE

There are three ways to monetize market research: sell data, sell technology, or sell services.

Let's talk about how to make money—

…As a Data Company

Data companies generally amass as much information as they can on their area of specialty. More likely than not, it is a form of measurement data that provides sales figures, marketing stats, consumer segmentations, or telemetry data. Once collected, they store it in some form of gigantic database to be parceled out as needed.

Almost every client wants some kind of limited segment of the data; few want to purchase the database in its entirety. Some clients may want the data month-by-month, some want it daily, and others want custom parameters, such as new products launched in the last twelve months or all the data pertaining to Australia.

Traditionally, clients would receive this in a static report (generally in the form of spreadsheets, ranging from the miniscule to the massive) that they were expected to load into their own information systems (or just trusty ol' Microsoft Excel). Sadly, little has changed, even among more established companies. Despite the capabilities of better technology and accessibility options, they still deliver "flat files" via email, FTP, or some other tool that requires their customers to do the heavy lifting.

In other words, the burden to extract the greatest value from the data rests on the shoulders of the party who knows the least about it.

The good news: more forward-thinking companies have challenged this. In addition to the examples I gave of Hoovers and Factual.com, almost every new data startup is leveraging interface technology and embracing the high-availability, delivery-on-demand models. The details vary: some charge by the number of data requests, by the number of categories available, the recency of the data, or the usage type of the data (ex. internal-only versus for commercial purposes).

However, one necessity remains consistent. In order to create a highly scalable data business, the data must to be easy to integrate and easy to access. Companies who continue to foist proprietary data-retrieval tools on their customers or who provide only static data views will soon find themselves at odds with their clients' internal data leaders who want to maximize the value of the data they buy.

... AS A TECHNOLOGY COMPANY

Microsoft, Oracle, IBM, and Sun have dominated the database technology field since virtually the inception of modern computing.

Massive clusters of computers that leveraged their database software systems have powered everything from banking services to high school grade records. As the Goliaths of data management software, these companies are experiencing the transitional pains of software commoditization as the market shifts under the weight of Big Data.

Hadoop, Mongo, Cassandra, Hive: they sound like names out of a sci-fi thriller. These companies are just a handful of new database technologies operating from the Open Source community that are taking millions of dollars away in software licensing from the Goliaths while simultaneously delivering data storage and analysis capabilities previously unobtainable. These low- or no-cost software systems empower commercial companies built on their offerings—such as Teradata, Cloudera, and Amazon—to host, process and store unlimited amounts of analytics-related data.

(…and I do mean *unlimited*.)

Mike Olson, CEO of Cloudera, believes that the business opportunity for the management of Big Data is at least as big as the market for data collection itself.

Companies like Cloudera are creating systems so that data queries that usually take hours can be done in a few minutes—or even seconds! The size of the data produced is not the primary issue. As we covered, moving a few gigabytes of data can happen quickly and cost effectively today. But the database systems that can perform these enormous processing requests are another story.

Companies who can undertake these challenges are now one of the technology start-up scene's hottest areas of growth. Silicon Valley venture capital firms have been very busy because they, too, see the potential. They want to be part of the action when the next Oracle or Microsoft appears. It is an exciting time to be in market research-related technology.

Right now, there are three key emerging technology products: blank slate data frameworks, tailored data frameworks, and rich-data products.

Blank slate technology companies provide the core technology for other companies to collect and manage data. Some of these have been around for a long time, like Microsoft SQL Server, Oracle, MicroStrategy, or Cognos. Others are more recent, such as Tableau, AnaMetrix, GoodData, and DoMo. These systems provide just the platform, assuming that the customer has the knowledge and ability to use it effectively. What is exciting about recently developed frameworks is that they are designed from the ground up with data connectivity in mind. These systems leverage "data connectors," systems where access to many technology interfaces from various data vendors are pre-built so that they can receive content directly into the central dashboard with minimal friction.

Josh James, founder and CEO of DoMo Technologies, is one of the forerunners in the delivery of data connector-driven, cloud-based business intelligence services. James believes that a paradigm shift is underway as consumers of information discover that they can have real-time data from any source of information they have access to. At the Web 2.0 Summit in 2011 he summed it up nicely: "Over $10 billion has been invested into the conventional wisdom that business intelligence is working for companies. The conventional wisdom is wrong." Clearly, investors agree with him: DoMo raised over $100 million in funding between 2010 and 2013 in support of their different vision for the industry.

But these companies offer only a blank slate. While they have some pre-configured widgets, charts, and recommendations for layout, you still need internal employees or consultants to connect all the relevant data, develop the layouts, and maintain the reporting. But these new technologies are a huge leap forward in the direction of contextual analysis. The only thing they are missing is the attribution and identity data necessary to allow internal analyses versus market analyses. For the most part, they are all largely still focused on providing access to internal operations and efforts.

(For now.)

Tailored technology companies are a variant on these new blank slate systems. Take EEDAR's tailored technology offering, GamePulse, for example. This business insights system not only supports clients who wish to load data on their own internal products, but also supplies data from external sources for competitors products. This enables the client to perform contextual analyses beyond the myopia of their own world and look to a larger universe that provides insights on the total market. Beyond the data, GamePulse delivers an immediate, out-of-the-box suite of analysis tools, pre-made reports, and layouts "tailor made" to meet the unique needs of the video game industry.

The purpose behind tailored technologies is to remove that last mile of friction that usually exists between business intelligence services and the end user, via interfaces that immediately provide 90% of their needs. The remaining 10% of their needs generally represent fringe cases that come up from time to time. For those, the end user can use built-in tools for an ad hoc analysis.

Tailored technologies are the next logical step for current blank slate companies as they penetrate deeper into specific markets. They generally do not scale as well as blank slate platforms since they are niched. However, they are more highly valued by their targeted users, are more rapidly adopted, and can generate higher revenue per client than their blank slate counterparts.

It is exciting that blank slate and tailored technologies allow companies to perform better and more contextual analyses than previously possible. But perhaps even more exciting are the companies using the same data to power consumer-facing tools and services—that is, **rich data technologies.**

One of the most pervasive, yet least known, uses of rich data technology is in the form of "interest-based advertising," also known as "retargeting." Interest-based advertising is the reason why, after you go to the BMW website to dream about that shiny new car, it seems that every website you go to over the next few days features an ad about cars, car loans, or car accessories. Simply put, certain websites share data with each other to tailor ads to each consumer's specific and recent interests.

For example, a few weeks ago I realized I needed some new business shirts. I had in mind a particular no-iron, no-wrinkle shirt that I had purchased once before. It worked perfect for day trips to San Francisco (in that I could show up at meetings without looking like I had been through a plane ride). After purchasing a few shirts from an online retailer, I continued browsing the web. Immediately, I began to see advertisements across a wide range of web sites for various no-iron, no-wrinkle shirts I might like. Of course, the data behind the system was incomplete. Had I not already made the purchase, I might have perceived the ads as cool. Since I had already bought the shirts, the ads quickly became annoying.

But imagine if the retargeting software were connected to a contextual analysis framework. It would gather such information as the color shirts I prefer, whether I like American cotton or Egyptian, and if I gravitated toward solid colors or stripes. If it also knew whether I had already made a purchase somewhere and if I had spent over, say, $500, the software could have advertised related products: a belt or jacket that would go nicely with my new shirts, or a watch priced appropriately to my shirt purchase.

Rich data services are everywhere: from Netflix for movie recommendations to Kayak for cheap airfares. The pervasiveness of data allows all kinds of services to be smarter and more predictive. As we move toward the Internet of Everything, it provides an enormous opportunity for market research companies who can empower consumer companies with smart technologies.

… AS A SERVICE COMPANY

With data measurement companies and technology companies, there is minimal human involvement between the data and the client who purchases the data. Overall, these two categories offer the highest profit margins because once the company breaks even on development costs, they simply resell a virtually identical product or technology over and over again.

Service companies, on the other hand, are defined by one simple rule: the products cannot be delivered without a human being involved. They could be a third-party consultant or even an internal department providing analysis to the rest of the organization.

This area is where the majority of market research work has traditionally resided: qualitative, quantitative, conjoint, custom studies, concept testing, and consulting. More often than not, the deliverable is a report of some kind, perhaps with data tables attached, that answers whatever question or goal the client requested.

This business segment exists because service providers can often do a better job than the client, for whatever reason: cost effectiveness, lack of personal knowledge, lack of capability, or simply a lack of time. Of course, service businesses come with their own host of issues.

Over my career I have developed a number of product lines that are service-based. I personally think it is one of the most rewarding aspects of the market research business, since it means direct interaction with clients and learning more about their businesses. From time to time, though, I engage in a common discussion when dealing with new customers (or new divisions within existing clients). After going through all the usual steps of the product engagement, a conversation ensues that goes something like this:

"Yeah, so overall we liked most of the report, but we had some follow-up questions."

"Sure, go ahead."

"Well, we were wondering who specifically worked on the report?"

"It was worked on by a number of our analysts. Was there a specific concern?"

"Well, we were just wondering, because some of our people disagree with the conclusions. We want to make sure that the person who worked on it actually understood our product properly. Otherwise, the report isn't really that useful."

Almost always, their lines of questions have little to do with actually understanding who worked on the report. More often than not, their questions reflect that the report contained some piece of information they did not necessarily want to deal with. Service companies are generally well prepared to address the qualifications of their analysts. In the case of EEDAR, analysts go through a year long training program (on top of their inherent skills and experience), before they are deemed competent to work with all the products they could be exposed to in our industry. But what has proven to be the most effective way to address qualification questions isn't showcasing a training regimen. Rather, it is by ensuring conclusions are logically derived from contextual data.

As a service company, it is critical to be as transparent as possible. The more information is obscured, the easier it is for clients to disagree with the deliverables as opinions instead of as facts—something you definitely want to avoid if your intention is to build trust and loyalty over a long-term relationship.

A key aspect in resolving both the scalability and trust issues in a service-oriented research company is providing richer data and a contextual interpretation of the conclusions in any given project. When EEDAR rolled out the GamePulse system as a technology product, they did not just do it for external customers. Their service teams were also an enormous customer for this product. The ability to demonstrate strong contextual data for each finding in a report not only reduced any analyst subjectivity, but also educated clients on how they could utilize those data sets within their own day-to-day decisions more effectively.

One of the most rewarding aspects of operating a service business is when you see a client's eyes light up with that "click" of understanding: not just about the isolated conclusion in that specific moment, but how they can now use that newfound knowledge in future decision making.

... By Delivering Maximum Value

Regardless of whether your organization is a data provider, technology company, or service organization, the core question is this: how do you deliver maximum value?

Data itself has no inherent value. It's just simply dead numbers on a white background, worthless in and of itself. Value is extracted only when the data is utilized. When a marketing team changes their positioning as a result of their research activities, then the data has delivered value. When a CEO changes a company's strategy because of trend information indicating they are failing, the data has delivered value.

Logically then, maximum value is achieved via maximum utility. That utility comes in two parts. The first is how actionable the information is; the second is how often the information can be acted upon. The more you enable your clients to use your information, and the more often they can do so, the more valuable you become to them.

With contextual analysis systems set to become a foundational element of market research, the value of data will soon come under much higher scrutiny. For data to be actionable, it must meet a host of ever increasing standards. Is the data trustworthy? Will the provider still be in business in five years? Was the data collected legally? Is it comprehensive enough? Will it work with our other data systems?

Creating the high quality data that will power future contextual analysis systems is going to be expensive and, until it becomes the industry standard, remain somewhat hard to justify for many vendors' potential clients. (Hopefully, this book will give you some ammunition for that fight, either within your organization or with your clients.) Data consumers will need more education to truly understand the value of the best data available—albeit expensive—versus good-enough data.

One way to mitigate the financial decision is for data curation companies to partner with contextual analytics technology companies. By proactively creating synergistic relationships, these companies can work together to increase the quality of information available to their mutual clients. In fact, as these data and technology synergies continue to blossom, the value of all the data in the contextual framework rises exponentially.

The need for such partnerships became very apparent early in the design phase of EEDAR's contextual analysis technologies. When I first began talking with the various measurement data providers in the video game industry, many were opposed to the idea. However, with the aid of mutual clients—and through long negotiations—I was able to move all of us past the historically competitive mindsets into relationships that have allowed effective "coopetition" with one another. The investment in establishing these relationships continues to deliver enormous dividends: the vendors who allow their data to operate as a part of the contextual framework see higher adoption rates with new potential clients, as well as increased retention rates with existing clients. While there has been some areas where companies lost business to one another in some of their overlapping product or service areas, the overall approach has allowed each company to focus on their areas of strength. Ultimately, our mutual clients have been clear winners: they get higher quality components that work together seamlessly in a more powerful research ecosystem.

THE RISING TIDE FOR BOUTIQUE VENDORS

This underscores one of my firmest beliefs about the future of market research: the commoditization of data, combined with the capabilities between datasets to work together, is going to shift the market away from mediocre data providers to those who provide the highest quality.

While contextual analysis supports the integration of all qualities of data, over time "good-enough" data will not provide the depth and accuracy necessary to fulfill the maximum potential this methodology affords. As a result, I believe that with contextual frameworks permeating multiple industries, the business of market research will embrace the capabilities of highly focused boutique shops that offer the most actionable information for their verticals.

Once they are established, new entrants in those spaces will find it difficult to unseat them (provided the incumbents continue to do a decent job). In my experience, clients quickly become accustomed to working with the best providers in a niche. Once they have established a true synergy with that provider in their contextual analytics framework and understand the value of the insights they have access to, those clients are unwilling to accept lower quality data, even if the cost savings are substantial. They understand that cheaper data comes at a steep price.

The market research business is a long-term play. Executives often make multimillion-dollar decisions based on the data they have. If that research is not accurate, their decisions could cost them their entire business. Unsurprisingly, they want to work with companies who have established themselves, with whom they have a great relationship, who they can trust, and who deliver the best value possible.

Leonard Murphy, Chief Editor of the Greenbook Research Industry Trends Report, provided some interesting insights in the Winter 2013 study. He found that data clients spending under $250,000 a year on research typically focus on data suppliers' price points and reputation. From there to $750,000 a year, clients focus more on suppliers' experience and consultative skills, especially concerning how long they have been in business and how well they can understand their needs. For clients spending over $1 million a year, they look for suppliers who can provide the highest quality delivery, are financially stable, and can adapt as rapidly as their business needs do.

Simply put, the most viable business model is to have a best-in-class product nobody else can compete with, focused on a unique niche you can serve very, very well. Thus, contextual analytics offers not only a way to provide more value to your clients, but a way to create an ecosystem that effectively shuts out all but the most serious of competitors—and even them you can turn into your coopetition.

But if you overreach by trying to do too much and be all things to all people, you will sacrifice quality on some front. The moment you compromise the quality of your products and services, you create an opportunity for someone else to step in and establish a foothold.

10
COST VS. VALUE WITH CONTEXTUAL ANALYTICS

The voyage of discovery is not in seeking new landscapes,
but in having new eyes.

—Marcel Proust

Good, fast, cheap: pick any two.

The "triple constraint" is dreaded by decision-makers in businesses everywhere. It is also known as the "Iron triangle" because it is seen as unbreakable. You can have a low price and high quality, but at a snail's pace; high quality at a fast pace but a steep price; or a low price at a fast pace, at the sacrifice of quality.

Yet another reason contextual analytics is such a groundbreaking concept is that it can break the iron triangle for information consumers by delivering high quality information, quickly, at a competitive price vis-à-vis competing methodologies. (Okay, "break" may be too dramatic of a term. Let's say contextual analytics "bends" the triangle.)

Yes, you have upfront costs. EEDAR, for instance, invests heavily in developing proprietary research tools and creating previously nonexistent datasets. Developing the initial classification hierarchy and dataset took years before it could be commercialized. But once the core infrastructure is in place for a particular market segment, you can enable additional datasets to work within that structure quite cost effectively. As you introduce each new dataset, the value of the entire framework then increases exponentially.

As more companies adopt a contextual analytics approach and provide consistent attribution and identity data, it will become even easier for everyone else in the industry to work with the disparate sets of information. In almost every business and industry, there is an enormous backlog of attribution data that needs to be manually curated. Eventually, though, the focus will shift from manually cataloging what exists to slicing and dicing the data as soon as it exists, enabling a whole new array of technology and service offerings to emerge.

But all of that data does not magically work together. Analysts cannot simply copy-paste rows of data into an Excel spreadsheet and suddenly reveal the mysteries of the universe. Enabling those datasets to work together requires painstaking effort to catalog the metadata. At any given time, fully half of EEDAR's labor hours are devoted to identifying product attributes. The data they create simply is not available anywhere else. To drill down to the level of clarity clients need, EEDAR has to do the hard work themselves (at considerable expense).

This is still the primary challenge in adopting a contextual approach. With this type of analytics still in its infancy, the needed layers of metadata do not exist for the vast majority of products, even in well-established industries. Data vendors' typical approach limits attribution data to cover only a portion of the products available on the market—say, the top fifty, or only those released by the three biggest players. Contextual analytics requires data on as many products as possible—ideally, the entire market—because it is critical to know which factors are reliably present in instances of success *and* failure.

Thomas Edison purportedly said, "I have not failed. I have just found 10,000 ways that don't work." Data on all products is critically important because sometimes there is not much separating what sells and what fails. If you do not have the complete picture, then how can you separate the signal from the noise?

The Price of Inertia

Putting aside the direct costs for a moment, let's look at the opportunity costs of *not* adopting a contextual analytics approach.

After chairman Alan Greenspan left the Federal Reserve, we learned that he watched the market for cardboard boxes as a proxy economic indicator. Since everything from shoes to electronics to washing machines comes in a cardboard box, a rise in demand reflects a rise in production that, in turn, reflects an expectation of more economic activity (or so the reasoning goes). There are plenty of other and far more bizarre economic indicators, such as the Big Mac Index,

Sports Illustrated Cover Indicator, and Hemline Index that all seem to correlate at times with how the economy performs. The people who accurately predict the economy's movement make millions of dollars with their prophetic foreknowledge manipulating futures, shorts, and other financial wizardry. But like Alan Greenspan, their genius comes from carefully watching certain indicators and acting on information before everyone else does.

How much would a CEO pay to know where their own market would be in a year? Six months? In some industries, even six weeks would allow them to make a killing. The companies continually at the forefront of their market are those like Alan Greenspan, examining twenty, thirty, or fifty different indicators to gauge where their market is headed. Such indicators could range from the number of people using golf driving ranges in a region, to how many bottles of aspirin were sold last week, to the GDP of certain countries. Every factor that remotely affects a company's products and services has some degree of contextual relevance.

But if senior executives have no way to see those indicators, they are flying blind.

Companies that adopt a contextual approach and enable their internal data to quickly and effectively work with the other datasets at their disposal will jump light-years ahead of their competition in response to market changes. If Yahoo! and AOL had examined a number of different website usage statistics, they might have concluded that people wanted less, not more, on their screens and have competed with Google (on that aspect, at least) instead of being relegated to obscurity in the search engine business. Had airlines looked beyond the airports where they operated, they might have spotted the opportunity Southwest Airlines seized on, flying to smaller airports in a point-to-point system instead of the traditional hub-and-spoke. While Southwest continues to be profitable, many of its larger competitors have gone bankrupt.

It is incredibly rare that market changes that appear to happen overnight actually do happen that quickly. There are almost always signs early on that, in hindsight, were glaringly obvious signals of a market shift. But if the company's executives have no practical way to get those signals, can we blame them for playing catch-up? How could they be expected to be proactive?

Take for example the 2008 global financial crisis. Many people were shocked and surprised as many of the world's economies fell to tatters, homes were foreclosed on, and banks verged on collapse. But it is incredibly difficult to imagine why we—and especially the leaders of nations and global financial institutions—could not see it coming.

Way back in 1998, the U.S. passed legislation to allow regular banks and investment banks to operate in conjunction with one another. Shortly after the first dot-com bust in 2000, the Federal Reserve lowered interest rates severely, thereby devaluing anything currency-based. This forced asset managers to look to new ways to generate income outside of traditional currency-based investments such as bonds. So they turned to mortgage-backed securities that, for reasons still unknown, were given AAA credit ratings...even though they were high-risk investments that had been considered "junk" for years. Fund managers purportedly relied on these credit ratings to begin large-scale investing. After the SEC made exemptions to allow the five largest Wall Street banks to operate with unlimited leverage restrictions, it left almost no room for error.

In 2004, the laws preventing many predatory lending practices in many states were overridden by a federal regulation, resulting in a spike in high-risk lending by smaller, unregulated banks. This created a swath of new mortgage products to take advantage of the new regulatory environment. These new financial products were quickly adopted by many of the larger commercial banks so they could remain competitive vis-à-vis the less-regulated small entities. All of that led to an influx of new and largely unqualified buyers. Many of these consumers held loans set to automatically increase after just a few short years.

That segment eventually hit critical mass…about the same time the housing bubble finally burst. As defaults rose and house prices fell, the system collapsed on itself. According to *Forbes*, by the time the bubble burst, the financial ecosystem built on these conditions exceeded three times the global economy on paper.

Politics and ideals aside, the reality of this perfect storm forming should have been foreseen—and certainly should have been seen in real-time. But the storm had already struck before the world markets knew what hit them.

The tragedy is that all of this could have been avoided with smarter data.

This, perhaps, is the real value behind contextual analytics. With the ability to make disparate sets of data effectively work together, analysts can gain insights into what is happening as it happens. More importantly, the systems can often provide immediate insight into *why* something is happening.

Without this—a framework that enables a true contextual analysis—researchers will continue to work with data that is months or even years old, unable to see the coming storm until it has already hit home.

THE COST VERSUS MONEY ALREADY BEING SPENT

We have covered the relatively expensive costs of adopting a contextual approach, but plenty of companies already budget sufficient funds to do so.

According to the International Broadcasting Convention (IBC), by 2016 the market research industry will be worth an estimated $50.7 billion—over 500% growth from the humble $8.1 billion it was back in 2006. Companies are already spending enormous sums of money, and apparently are planning to spend even more. But as I have demonstrated, buying more information does not necessarily mean being more informed, nor does it mean companies are getting smarter about the way they invest their research dollars.

Some companies could opt for a contextual approach simply by shifting their budget from buying multiple and duplicative datasets within a single measurement type to buying a diverse collection of datasets that work together within a contextual analysis framework.

One of the key advantages we find is that instead of isolated initiatives where only one or two budget pools contribute to the total expenditure, contextual analytics can offer multiple departments insights from the entire ecosystem of the product's lifecycle. That, in turn, often means the costs can come from multiple departments' budgets. Together, everyone receives higher quality and more comprehensive insights than they would by working separately.

Take UPS for example. The delivery company created an attribution layer to link its disparate datasets from its onboard truck data, GPS data, and its logistics database. This contextual approach allowed UPS to redraw its delivery routes, shaving off some eighty-five million miles. As a result, the company saw millions of dollars in cost savings due to using less fuel; lower vehicle leases; less maintenance; and reduced labor hours of drivers, mechanics, and route planners. Even warehouse operations benefited from the higher efficiency of delivery operations. Just linking a few already-available datasets had an enormous impact across the company's entire business.

From a budget perspective, the project could have been paid for solely out of business intelligence. However, there would also have been a solid justification for covering part of the cost with the operations budgets from logistics, transportation, maintenance, and project management. If each of those four areas contributed 25% of the cost of creating a contextual framework, they would each have considered the resulting insights a bargain—and the business intelligence department could have used their own untouched budget to add additional datasets to that ecosystem, thereby extracting even more value from it.

I have yet to find a company where the total cost of ownership in creating a contextual analytics framework could not be accomplished within their existing budget. The problem is that their research budgets are decentralized and operating independently of each other. By aligning their research projects and getting the different efforts to work in tandem, my clients extract far higher value with the same overall research investment.

In short, companies can save millions just as they can make millions with contextual analytics. In my professional experience, the total cost in developing and maintaining a contextual analysis system delivers returns-on-investment in excess of 500% within the first year of deployment for company's able to fully embrace the potential it provides.

Yes—contextual analytics is worth it.

The Benefit of Enabling Innovation (Or Not)

I have a client in Europe who I get together with from time to time. Somehow, we always fall into some discussion on the relevance of market research, with each of us coming from the opposite point of view. One of our longest-running debates is whether or not market research can truly be used for innovation.

I promise, after two or three beers, it is riveting stuff.

His side of the argument is what I refer to as the Henry Ford position. Legend has it that Ford once said, "If I had asked people what they wanted, they would have said faster horses." My client makes a good case. Historically, people's opinions are excellent at revealing what has already occurred, but remarkably poor at predicting what's to come. Steve Jobs did not create the iPhone because customers asked for a computer that they could make calls with. Rather, he intuitively created what he knew they would want once they understood what it did.

I understand my debate partner's position: customer survey data has little in the way of innovation-related insights because the customers themselves are exposed to little in the way of cutting-edge products, services, and ideas. The things that everyday people interact with are…well, everyday things. Even if, by lucky chance, a survey sample does include a few people with truly new ideas, the sample size is so small that few executives want to act on it. Essentially, they would be betting the success of their company and their reputation on the opinions of just a few dozen people.

For companies who want to create disruptive products and services like Apple did with the iPhone, Tesla with electric cars, BitCoin with digital currencies, or TiVo with the DVR, the past offers few clues. Real innovation in the vein of these companies must necessarily come from looking beyond the constraints of consumers' (or even competitors') ideas. (Or so my friend argues as we down another beer.)

How I wish I could refute his point and bring out an example with such a flourish and finality that it would leave him gasping for breath. Alas, despite a diligent search, the strongest argument I can offer is that data *could* reveal insights leading to disruptive innovation…*if* people knew how to use it right.

In *The Innovator's Dilemma*, Clayton Christiansen says that innovation comes from one of two things. The first is called the low-end: existing products made relevant for the niche markets that bigger companies do not want to serve. Craft beer, for instance, remained a niche market for quite some time, though it is now finally becoming mainstream. Low-end disruption simply repurposes a technology for a specific market, if you will. In this type of disruptive innovation, which is more about exploiting price gaps and market leaders' laziness, market research is perhaps the most powerful tool available.

On the other hand, the second type of disruptive innovation occurs when barriers that have heretofore prevented consumers from engaging with a product or service can be effectively removed. I would argue that amongst all of these, while technology is often the most looked at barrier in modern days that empowers disruptive innovation, the truly amazing changes occur when *social* barriers are removed. While the world identifies the iPhone as a revolutionary product, the truth is that its components had been around for years. Smartphones like BlackBerrys and Windows application-running devices existed. The internet had been around for quite some time. We could download applications onto our phones (remember the AT&T marketplace on those old cell phones from the 90s?). The early adopters of smartphones, though, were computer nerds savvy enough to work all that. Steve Jobs simply created a user experience that not only made all those things accessible to us in a single device, but he turned the social economy on its head by making it cool to own one.

Furthermore, the iPhone was really just a marriage of existing devices: an iPod, a cell phone, a GPS navigator, a web browser, and a storefront where people could download customizable software add-ons for their device via the internet. Prior to the iPhone's entrance, music device manufacturers were focused only on figuring out how to produce better MP3 players. The cell phone industry was focused only on how to make better batteries or faster transmission speeds. The GPS industry was focused only on how to improve the next clunky device to plug into a car's cigarette lighter. Steve Jobs created billions of dollars in value for Apple when he thought, *Hey, even if no one component were the best, wouldn't people prefer to have all of these functions in one easy-to-use device that fit in your pocket?*

If someone else had been able to link the rising popularities among consumers across these disparate industries—music, navigation, cameras, PDAs, etc.—and identified the common threads that pointed toward a future intersection of them all, Apple may have been playing catch-up instead of leading the field. Of course, Steve Jobs's innovative products came more from his intuition than any data. So this example still does not disprove my client's Henry Ford argument…but it points to how companies *could* use market research to do so.

So both my friend's Henry Ford argument and my own have merit. Unsurprisingly, this mirrors the debates in companies across the globe. Some believe listening to customers will lead to inertia (à la Zynga), while others believe not listening to their customers will lead them to their doom (à la Qwikster). In creative industries, some people engage in a parallel argument around design: some want complete artistic control, devoid of any information that might taint their creative expression, while others wholly embrace "commercial art" and leave little room for creativity.

There is no easy solution to how looking back helps you look forward. True innovation, by its very nature, requires an element of creative genius and inspiration. However, contextual analytics gives us new tools that can inform us. The ability to draw upon multiple and diverse data sources can guide us to deeper research, better questions, and more relevant decisions to help us explore the unknown.

11

THE ROAD TO
CONTEXTUAL ANALYTICS

It is not necessary to change. Survival is not mandatory.
—W. Edwards Deming, statistician and professor

In the course of my day-to-day business, I encounter dozens of companies that span the gamut of the market research vendors.

Telemetry companies that track billions of transactions a day. Survey companies seeking to unlock consumer behavioral insights. Attribution companies collecting rich information on products. Technology companies with amazing software frameworks or modeling capabilities. Consulting companies with enough Ph.Ds. to open their own university.

Quite frankly, whether you are a data vendor, technology vendor, or service vendor, the rise of contextual analytics is the largest opportunity in decades to expand the total market research industry while delivering value to clients at an unprecedented level. Sadly, many companies will continue to hoard their precious data or technical capabilities, trying to wring out a few more drops of perceived competitive advantage while their competitors swim forward in an ocean of insight.

But what if you are part of a market research vendor further along this path—someone who already works with multiple sets of data and wants to know how to go from where you are to a full-scale contextual analytics company? There is so much opportunity in the world of market research that it is easy to lose focus. If you want to establish a viable business model—and especially if you see the necessity of evolving toward contextual analytics—your company must step back and ask the most esoteric of all questions.

"Who are we?"

What role do you fill in market research? What do you ostensibly provide? What do you *actually* provide? To whom are you trying to sell?

As we have explored, the market is moving toward high specialization. Very few companies will survive the attempt to be all things to all people. The trick, then, is to identify the segment in which you can be the absolute best. So, all you have to do is find the place where you can deliver the highest quality data, technology, and/or services.

(No problem, right?!)

The first step centers on recognition (and sometimes admission) of what business you are truly in. You may realize you sit primarily on the attribution and identity tier, even if you also perform some level of analysis. On the other hand, you might conduct business more at the monetization tier, collecting very little data yourself. Or, you might fit in elsewhere on the spectrum, focusing more on measurement data or even analyst education. Where you currently find your company is less important than simply making sure you know where that is. Otherwise how else can you know what pieces you still need to add to the puzzle?

Once you know that, you can ask questions about your ecosystem. What is your strategy for identity management? How can you create unique identities for all these datasets? How do you plan to homogenize the data? How will the attribution layer function to enable all these pieces to work together? Where is all the data coming from?

Then comes the question of what technologies should be in place. Will all this data spit out just one report? Should you create a dynamic web portal where people can manipulate the data at will? Should you support dynamic modeling or require customers to utilize their own? Any combination of approaches may work, and the way different companies answer these questions will create a wide variety of unique products for the market research industry.

Lastly is the question of build, buy, or partner. In order to create a contextual analysis ecosystem, your company may choose to outsource data collection and focus instead on delivering technology or services. Or you may mix and match. You might even decide to go the other direction and focus on dataset creation and hire other vendors to do the software engineering for you. There is no exact path. Each company is unique.

Ultimately though, the key to being successful as a market research vendor in the new age of contextual analysis will come down to this: how is your organization ensuring that your customers receive maximum value from what you are providing? Because if someone else can deliver a superior solution—and they will, as anyone who has ever rested on their laurels knows—a twenty-year client relationship will only delay the inevitable.

EVOLVING ... AS A DATA COMPANY

At risk of belaboring an earlier point: the data vendor business is moving away from price as a differentiator to quality as the differentiator—for every type of company. Your company must choose to either offer the absolute best quality data that works within a greater contextual framework or become a commodity company operating on razor thin margins.

(I am assuming you want the former and to avoid the latter, correct?)

So how can your company begin the transition? The first challenge is the lack of products' identity. That is, how can you make your disparate datasets—collected at different levels of abstraction, identifying products in different ways, curated in some cases and crowdsourced in others—all align and work together? For now, the answer is DIY: do it yourself.

Until your respective business segment creates a set of standard conventions, your company must develop and maintain, from scratch, your own identity management system and tools. Depending on how far you want to take it, this identity system could be an enormous investment.

At EEDAR, for instance, about half of all the total research efforts undertaken are identity-related. Every time a new vendor comes in, every time an existing vendor changes their data formats, and every time someone upgrades their technology components, a contextual analytics company has to re-evaluate and potentially alter its identity systems and data. Since that is often so time-consuming, few organizations choose to do this internally.

There are a handful of organizations out there that have undertaken the challenge. The international not-for-profit association GS1 holds the distinction as the most widely used system in the world for identity management. It has a number of product tracking systems designed to be appropriate for the various categories they serve, even while remaining centralized in a single master system. Despite their impressive efforts, their systems still cover only a fraction of the total products and systems needed.

No one at companies like GS1 should be concerned about job security for a very, very long time.

Evolving ... As a Technology Company

There is still an opportunity for companies to build out blank-slate solutions, particularly for those who can leverage open-source technologies and provide offerings on a more attractive licensing basis than the traditional companies. (Trust me, that won't be hard at current market rates.) Additionally, companies that can focus on improving the speed at which data can be transmitted, aggregated, or retrieved will have high appeal in coming years.

But don't wait too long. The promising field of data-related technology will eventually cool off. Cloud-based systems were the most recent major revolution in this space, and there are not many radical data storage or transmission revolutions left that are likely to occur before the year 2050. Always-on, high-speed, global internet via wireless systems? That will probably happen. Near unlimited portable power with new battery technologies, such as graphene? That will probably happen too. But aside from technology that will ostensibly only create more data to deal with, we are rapidly nearing the end of this period of inventing and shifting to one of refining. The technology revolution is nearly over and the real information age has begun.

While blank-slate tech will slow over time, tailored technologies will continue to flourish. Most of the tailored solutions will even require blank-slate technology to even exist. No matter how comprehensive the framework systems become, there will always be a need for industry-specific solutions. Tailored solutions will meet this insatiable thirst: merging the capabilities of all the data and technology that can be brought to bear with the expertise and passion individuals have for specific segments. This is the area of market research I expect will change the most over the next decade or two. Already, the companies I founded have demonstrated, in what is perhaps some of the most challenging industries to support today, that it is possible to create and maintain a comprehensive contextual analytics solution. It is only a matter of time before other industries begin to adopt similar approaches.

Let us not forget those companies with an eye toward applying contextual analysis to rich data technology. These are the systems that will be the most exciting to watch going forward. Companies that will have serious impact will be those who use contextual systems not just to support decision-making for their organization, but also to leverage contextual systems to power consumer-facing products and services.

Let me provide a personal anecdote to demonstrate what I mean. On a brisk, wet, winter night I was out to dinner in San Francisco. We had all had a few drinks, and then started talking about getting a cab. We were at the edge of downtown where getting one would probably take at least fifteen minutes to track down. A friend across the table pulled out their phone and started up a small app that immediately filled with a map and icons of little black cars in our vicinity. A few touches and swipes later, and one of the icons began zooming toward us. When the icon stopped on the map at our location, we all got up, walked out the door, and stepped into the waiting car. It was the most efficient inner-city transport experience I had ever had. I have been using that app, Uber, ever since!

A number of companies around the world now offer this service (much to the chagrin of local taxi companies who could have delivered this type of capability years ago if they operated with the customers in mind rather than the unions, drivers, and licensing boards). It uses a small number of datasets: in this case, GPS, a customer booking database, and a transaction system. Over time, it will only improve for the drivers as the providers add datasets from road construction, accidents, and real-time traffic to shorten trip times; convention, concert, or nightclub location highlighting to encourage increased car availability; and notifications when they are near the cheapest gas in town to help improve their profitability.

It doesn't stop there. After raising $258 million in 2013, Uber plans to purchase 2,500 automated vehicles (that's right—no driver required!) that leverage Google and Uber technologies to provide highly efficient transportation alternatives. It sounds sci-fi, but the "robo-taxi" is a reality.

EVOLVING ... AS A SERVICE PROVIDER

No matter how smart technology becomes, we are a long way from when artificial intelligence can interpret all the data and replicate the human thought process. Service vendors have one of the largest roles in helping companies navigate the deluge of information raining down on them. However, just because humans are still needed does not mean that they, too, do not need to evolve. The skills needed to be an effective service vendor are changing. It is getting harder and harder for small shops that have historically thrived solely on their personal experience and knowledge in a market segment to compete with companies utilizing data systems and analysts to provide objective, responsive insights to their customers. These "gut-instinct" providers will slowly fade away as the data-enabled consultant comes to the fore.

While it is certainly beneficial as a service provider to be looking at bringing data scientists, modelers, STATA gurus, or R programmers into your organization, contextual analytics does offer a bridge of sorts. While leveraging the full power of a contextual data ecosystem requires some technical skills your subject matter experts may lack, there is an enormous amount of information that can be obtained out of the box by using the frameworks to provide data visualization, segmentation, analysis, and reporting.

It is exciting when you can arm someone who has deep experience in your business with the data *and* capabilities they have dreamed of having for years. In order for anything like this to happen inside an existing company, however, someone has to become the internal champion for this approach.

We're talking about *you*.

PART IV

BEING A CHAMPION OF CHANGE

12

BEING A BETTER DATA CONSUMER

Some people use research
like a drunkard uses a lamppost;
for support, not illumination.
—David Ogilvy

A retail customer of mine called me out of the blue one morning and, after walking me through two similar datasets, asked me to tell her which one I thought she should purchase.

We discussed many of the principles covered in this book and she recognized that her business could actually benefit from both of them. However, the discussion kept coming back to her wanting to understand the difference in value between the two of them. One dataset was based on an observation methodology and more comprehensive. The other dataset was based on a sampling approach and, although less comprehensive, contained behavioral information the first one lacked.

After a half hour or so, she got to the crux of her dilemma: "I guess I'm just trying to figure out if it's worth paying for the more comprehensive one. I'd rather not buy both."

"Well," I countered, "how much is the decision worth that you're going to make based on using either of these datasets?"

"Well, it's hard to say exactly, but since it will impact every store to some degree, probably somewhere in the tens of millions."

"So is spending an extra $20,000 to have *both* datasets worth it when your decision is worth $20 million?"

She paused for a moment, then said, "I guess that puts it into perspective, doesn't it?"

And that was the end of that discussion.

Ask Smarter Questions as a Data Consumer

I get these types of phone calls all the time. Data purchasers often look so closely at cost management that they lose sight of the value of the decisions they will make based on that data. On the other hand, some people keenly understand data's importance, and consequently acquire multiple datasets representing the exact same information so they can feel confident that they have reliable data.

But in both scenarios, the data purchaser limits themselves. Buying only one dataset restricts you to only one perspective, but buying multiple datasets of the same type of data limits to you to one perspective, too. You need data from all three areas—supply, consumption, and discovery—to provide the total picture. Utilizing three different datasets that only report on sales at retail will not be able to reveal anything about how a marketing campaign impacted a customers' choice to purchase a paperclip in the first place (since your data does not even reflect that a marketing campaign occurred).

As a market research consumer, you have to be aware that while one type of data in isolation may be the most accurate you could possibly ask for, it provides only a fraction of its total value until you connect it into a data ecosystem and understand its context.

The moment your research focus shifts from "yes or no" questions, to "how" and "why" questions, one set of numbers cannot provide the answer by themselves. You have to have additional relevant datasets to provide context. The first task is to examine your entire inventory of information, categorize them by type into their various areas, and then ask yourself: "Where can we find the rest?"

Since we are still in the early stages of this new phase of market research, the datasets you need may not exist yet. For now, most companies will have to either direct their internal departments to start finding ways to capture and curate the data, or pay their data vendors to do it for them.

In any case, as a consumer of measurement data, here are many of the key questions you should ask:

- What type of information is being presented?

- With what methodology is the data collected?

- What other sets of data could it work with?

- Does the data available represent multiple aspects of the product lifecycle, or is it confined to just one?

- Is the product attribution data included collected internally, or purchased from a third party and merged into our own datasets? How accurate is it? Does it cover the entire market, or just a subset?

- Is the data provided in a way that makes it easy to link with other datasets we already have?

- What are the options available for how data is delivered?

On the technology side, you should be asking your vendors:

- Is this technology a blank-slate framework, tailored solution, or rich-data offering?

- Does the technology require any human involvement in connecting new datasets to it?

- Who is responsible for maintaining and updating any models or formulas the technology utilizes?

- How is the data stored? Will it grow as my total data size grows? What hardware do you supply, or do I need to buy, in order to support that?

- Does the system require any other licensing? Is it utilizing open source systems? Have all those systems been appropriately credited to avoid any legal exposures?

- How does the system leverage identity and attribution data to support dynamic market segmentation?

- How does the technology provide a contextual view of the data it presents: do I have to find it myself with multiple requests, or has it been tailored to do some of that already?

Of course, a list of questions on the technology front could go on much longer, but these are a good starting point and will certainly put any vendor on notice that, as a buyer, you are looking for richer value out of their offerings than they may have been used to providing before.

Let us not forget the largest category of vendors: service companies. Here are some of the most important questions you should be asking them as they complete each RFP you send out:

- What data are you using to perform the analysis? (For each data type you could then leverage data questions from above.)

- What technology are you using with the data in conjunction with the analysis? Do you leverage a contextual analytics framework? Is it a syndicated service you subscribe to, or an internal one that you have produced yourself?

- Explain the approach you take to ensure that your analysis is driven by facts and not by subjective opinions.

- In the event an area of interest arises from the initial research effort, how will you perform a deeper analysis? How long will that take to do? How much will it cost?

- What expertise do the analysts you have on staff bring to the research topic at hand? Are all your analysts internal, or do you leverage external consultants?

- If we are providing information to assist with the research, how is that being utilized? How is it being kept secure (if necessary)?

- How will the research be applicable in solving the needs we have at hand? How will it allow us to make the decisions we need to make?

Again, there are many more questions you might ask a service provider, but the key idea is to ensure that you get the most comprehensive, data-backed analysis possible that will deliver the appropriate value for the investment you make.

EXPAND, REUSE, AND RECYCLE YOUR DATA

Perhaps the most important question you should ask of every market research effort is: "Can this be used somewhere elsewhere within our organization?"

What is the likelihood that, throughout your entire company, your department is the *only* one who can extract value from the information? Virtually nil—yet you would be amazed how many five- and six-figure market research reports sit on people's desks collecting dust. Plenty of companies spend a small fortune to sponsor research projects, then discuss the results at a board meeting and never use the data again.

What a waste!

Any data your organization collects should be integrated into a central knowledge system of some kind. If it is raw data (of sufficient quality), then it can go into your contextual analytics ecosystem. If it is an ad hoc report, then it can go into a common library. At the very least, you should come up with some way to avoid the world's standard operating procedure: throwing it on a network drive and forgetting about it forever.

Microsoft has a powerful service they use to ensure that knowledge is centralized as much as possible throughout their organization. The aptly named Microsoft Library group works to ensure that any syndicated research or data that can be shared across departments is purchased on a licensing basis that allows it to be used throughout the organization. Teams work to ensure that the data is then classified or integrated to make it as accessible as possible. While this approach will add additional headcount to your operating budget, it is a sound investment for larger companies who have multiple people buying or creating datasets from various sources and vendors.

Recognize the "Swords" and the "Shields"

Like most people, you probably accept the fact that mass media bias exists. CNBC leans left. Fox leans right. *The Wall Street Journal* skews conservative. *The New York Times* skews liberal. Nearly everyone knows somewhat of a bias exists, but people think the news sources opposed to their own perspective are more biased than the ones they agree with. It is easy for conservatives to poke holes in a CNN documentary but harder for them to see the flaws in a similar Fox report (and vice versa for liberals).

Perhaps news sources should be required to have disclaimers: "87% of our journalists are registered Democrats," or "31% of our editors consider themselves independents." But after reading that disclaimer, would viewers or readers approach that news source any differently? Would they adjust their expectations, mentally warning themselves that what they were about to read or hear had an inherent bias?

Probably not. In fact, most people would likely use the information to reinforce what they already knew. Liberal voters would personally identify with the sources they already used; conservative voters would find conservative sources and use whatever they heard or read to do the same. The ugly truth is that most people find data to support the position they've already taken, and to either attack someone else's stance or to defend their own.

Unfortunately, the same is true when it comes to market research.

There is extensive academic literature indicating that many individuals make decisions initially at a subconscious level based on emotion or intuition, and then use their conscious mind to rationalize those decisions. In essence people often do actions or believe in ideas without any deliberate or logical process precipitating them. They simply decide first, and justify later. Unfortunately, much of the market research industry is driven by unscientific motives, too. Most market research professionals' experiences mirror this: many executives engage researchers having already decided on "the facts" and simply needing something to rationalize their decision. They start with the conclusion and then seek out data to justify it. Far too often, the people who commission market research projects want data that tells a specific story.

When I sit down with a potential client to kick off a research project, I can quickly discern when the marketing department just wants data to back up a decision they've already made or an executive wants information to justify their decision. Very few market researchers like these agenda-driven projects where the sponsor has already drawn their own conclusions, but across the industry this occurs on a regular basis.

From cigarettes to breast implants, "scientific studies" abound both for and against whatever is under the microscope. Recently my wife and I were driving to a restaurant and listening to the news. The reporter said, "A new study finds that sugar—" The reporter wasn't even finished before my wife declared, "I wonder who paid for that report!" It was quite the astute observation. It turns out that way back in 1968, the Sugar Association established the International Sugar Research Foundation (ISRF). From 1968-69 they spent $600,000 (about $4 million today) in research aimed to discredit the leading sugar alternative product of the time: cyclamate. By 1969, the FDA banned all cyclamates in the USA. Since that first victory, the ISRF has carefully walked the tightrope by supporting research that is specifically aimed at preventing negative scientific studies from translating into public policies.

In fact, as far back as 1976, the president of the Sugar Association at the time, John Tatem Jr., stated, "We try to never lose sight of the fact that no confirmed scientific evidence links sugar to death-dealing disease. This crucial point is the lifeblood of the association." Essentially, the whole point of the organization is to ensure that any negative research about sugar is discredited or, at the least, challenged on reliability. As recently as 2005 this had not changed. When new research emerged showing clear links between sugar and metabolic syndrome, a key cause of type-2 diabetes, the Sugar Association sent a newsletter to members noting that "any disparagement of sugar will be met with forceful strategic public comments and the supporting science."

(I imagine they'll support it with the science they paid to have produced.)

Market research costs money. So it is of little surprise that virtually no for-profit corporations commission it purely for the sake of academic enlightenment. That's the purview of universities! Simply, when someone invests money into an initiative they want a return on that investment.

A consequence of this book may well be an increase in your cynicism—but don't despair! That's the first sign you are becoming a more educated market researcher.

The Ideal Approach

If a purchaser of research always enjoys working with a vendor because the vendor always supplies findings that reinforce the purchaser's point of view—well, they have probably figured out the customer will keep paying them to tell him what they want to hear. As a consumer of any kind of data, you have a responsibility to ensure that, if the information comes back telling you something you did not want to hear, you are open to exploring why. As a provider of any kind of data, you have a responsibility to be able to clearly and effectively answer such a question with clarity (and, of course, good data).

The best (and rarest) research customer is the objective seeker of truth. They may have an agenda, but they are willing to modify or even abandon that agenda if the numbers tell them otherwise (assuming they trust them in the first place).

If you launch a research project with the question, "What answers do we want to get from this?", then more often than not, that is exactly what you will wind up with. The better approach is to ask, "What *questions* do we want answered from this?"

That way, the project minimizes bias from the very start. Instead of working toward what the recipient of the data wants to hear, the researchers work toward what the data reveals. When they present that information to the customer, it may not be what the customer wanted to hear, but it is what they wanted answered.

By beginning with the desired questions instead of the desired answers, the research team can gather context around those questions: "We don't understand how questions three and five fit together. Can you help us understand the connection between them?"

I often hear something like, "Last year we spent an average of $10 million marketing each product and we're considering spending an average of $12 million next year. We want to see if we should spend that extra $2 million."

In other words, will increasing their marketing budget by 20% result in increased sales? While that seems like a straightforward question, it assumes that their current marketing is the primary driver of their current sales. They initiated the research project by seeking an answer of yes/no.

I like to take a step back to explore what other factors influence their sales. Timing of release? Consumer engagement? Types and frequency of media utilized? Duration of campaigns? Quality of the advertisements? Lack of other competition at time of release?

The companies who get the most value welcome new information that helps them identify and create opportunities, allows them to understand the market better, supports their employees in being better informed, and substantially adds value to their thinking.

Sharp data consumers allow the data to inform their decisions—not the other way around.

13

BEING A DATA LEADER

Turn data into a point of view that makes sense for decision makers.
—Jean E. Engle, Chief Knowledge Officer,
NASA's Johnson Space Center

One day, I sat down to lunch with a client in charge of an e-commerce division for a Fortune 500 company. The priority of the division's market research centered on figuring out how much money went through their e-commerce platform and how to best reinvest that money into new market initiatives. On one hand, they needed to look at the past; on the other, to predict the future. They saw the potential in contextual analytics and wanted advice on how to best cull new opportunities out of the data they regularly pulled.

My client said, "Every week we pull up reports that show us, sector by sector, how our business is doing and compare that to previous periods to see if we've made more or less money. Some of the numbers we also look at include how many people have engaged in using our platforms. From that data, we have a review meeting and decide where we should be concentrating our future development efforts. After we meet, we send our recommendations off to the product development team and they determine which initiatives move forward."

I said, "That sounds interesting, but how do you identify possible opportunities outside of the internal data you have?"

He looked puzzled for a moment. "I don't understand your question."

"Well," I explained, "What you're doing is shifting resources from one product you already have to another product you already have. All your data is internal to your existing e-commerce products. You don't have any data from outside your vertical that indicates what other types of products are growing that might influence your platforms one way or another. I mean, you're in media—what other trends might be competing for your customers' attention? Where is the data trending for your core demographic? Are they spending more of their time and money elsewhere?"

"Oh," he said. "Hmmm. I guess I see your point, but that's not our responsibility to figure out."

"Well whose is it?" I asked.

"I…I don't know. I don't even know if there is anyone at our company who does that kind of research."

I pressed him: "But isn't your team responsible for going through all the data related to the platform and pulling it together?"

He said, "I guess so, but we don't have time to do that and everything else. All we have time to do is generate the reports for the product team."

Sadly, many of our clients recognize that their core demographic could be undergoing a major shift…and that the data to analyze it is available…and the potential discoveries could change their bottom line by millions of dollars … but, like my client here, they "are not responsible for that" or "don't have the time."

After all, they have to get their weekly reports out!

THE TASK BEFORE US

Far too often, too many employees are afraid to say anything that would be negatively received, despite the potential insanity of the ideas being contemplated. All over the world, internal analytics departments simply churn through the same types of data day after day because that is what their executives expect. They have little time to seriously dig into the data they have because they have to get out that next quarterly analysis. In doing so, they often miss a golden opportunity to truly analyze the data coming across their desks.

If you pointed out the shortcomings in some companies' internal reports, you would likely hear, "Yeah, well, it's great that you have an opinion on that, but this is the report they want, so…that's what I am going to give them." I spoke earlier about how some leaders are flying blind. With these analysts' companies, their leaders are *willfully* flying blind.

We can create products and services that do a better job of enhancing people's lives. With the sheer amount of data collected by businesses all over the world, with a comprehensive understanding of what people buy, by following what factors influence those decisions and to what degree, and by tracking how people spend their resources (notably time), we can be smarter about where we invest our time and money. We can save billions of dollars in wasted efforts in creating designs that ultimately get trashed, in spending millions on Super

Bowl ads that never earn a cent, and in manufacturing thousands of products no one ever buys. We can create billions of dollars' worth of value by identifying what factors correlate with better durability, in streamlining design and manufacturing processes to eliminate downtime and waste, and in perfectly matching consumers' tastes with what they want (instead of building it and hoping they will come).

It starts with "data leadership."

A Ground Floor Opportunity For Data Leaders

The market research industry and the business world in general—albeit reluctantly—understand that the future of wealth lies in information: finding it, collecting it, organizing it, analyzing it, and utilizing it. It is a complex task and the problem stems from the fact that there is so much of it. On top of that, every dataset can potentially link to thousands of others.

As a simple example, I demonstrated just how thick the web of data is around a simple paperclip. The sheer amount of information touching this one little piece of twisted wire boggles the mind. Where is all that information housed? In syndicated data sources...in some attorney's filing cabinet...in a marketing company's customer relationship database...in a production foreman's head...on a logistic company's webserver—all independent of each other.

If companies who want to be data-enabled do not have someone at the top organizing the data, uncovering insights, and representing the voice of data, how can anyone expect to take analytics seriously? Enter the newest—and fastest growing—corporate officer occupation across the public and private sectors: the Chief Data Officer.

In 2009, the FCC became the first federal agency to appoint CDOs in each division of the organization. At their head, Greg Elin took the reins in a tireless pursuit to ensure that all the FCC's data, both internal and external, was accessible and usable. His charter extends even beyond the data into ensuring that the technology and processes the data interacts with are also as efficient as possible. In short, he is catalyzing the adoption of a contextual analytics mindset within the FCC that will eventually lead them into operating within a contextual analytics framework.

A quick internet search for this new occupation of CDO will return a staggering number of results. The numerous appointments and job openings demonstrate how great the need is for professionals who can provide knowledge and direction on managing data within the company. Each of these positions has an enormous amount of work waiting for whomever fills it.

Market research service companies are growing at an astronomical rate as a result of the change taking place. After all, data needs to be turned into information in order for it to deliver value. In 2013, CNBC declared data analysts as the sexiest occupation of the twenty-first century! Rob Bearden, CEO of Hortonworks, expressed why: "The desire on the enterprise side to find truly qualified data scientists has resulted in almost open headcount. It's probably the biggest imbalance of supply and demand that I've ever seen in my career. ... The talent pool is, at best, probably 20% of the demand."

This rapid growth is not going unnoticed at the education level either, and a whole new generation is soon to arrive, trained from the ground up in data interpretation, statistics and modeling. At the 2013

International Olympiad of Informatics (yes there is an Olympics for data!), over 300 of the brightest minds in the world competed to solve incredibly challenging puzzles that leverage large datasets in a two-day competition. While 300 people competing may not sound like a large number, the Chinese team of 4 was selected from a pool of over 600,000 entrants who were whittled down to the best.

(China went on to sweep the competition, by the way.)

So with the cost structure of technology undergoing a sea change, the talent and skills of analysts on the rise, and the ever increasing amount of data needing to be turned into actionable information, there is only one way that existing data, technology, and service companies can avoid eventual extinction — by empowering their businesses to be friendly players within the world of contextual analytics.

Yes, there is a lot of work and plenty of expectations riding on the shoulders of those who fill these roles. Yet at the same, it offers a tantalizing opportunity for someone (hopefully like you) to take the reins and establish a culture of demanding more from your data. The market is undergoing an enormous shift on many fronts, and it is the perfect time to become the data leader your company needs you to be.

14

ACQUIRING TRUTH THROUGH CONTEXT

The truth is not for all, but only for those who seek it.
—AYN RAND

I distinctly remember my twenty-two-year-old trigonometry teacher, recently graduated from college, explaining the Pythagorean Theorem to a bunch of twelve-year-olds for the first time. At the end of the explanation, she said, "And this is why the Pythagorean Theorem is true."

Typical of high-schoolers, someone in the class asked, "Why?"

After a few frustrated attempts to supply an age-appropriate answer (we weren't quite ready for mathematical proofs), she finally said, "Pythagoras lived in Greece 2,500 years ago and was much smarter than all of us. So let's just accept that he was right and move on to the next exercise."

Essentially, she said, "Don't ask why and just accept it as Truth."

Looking back over my education, it was not until after I finished my undergraduate studies that there was ever much room to exercise my own opinion and still get top grades. Only a handful of subjects openly encouraged questioning the answers hitherto believed to be correct.

No wonder modern society is laden with such passive consumers.

We have been conditioned from a very young age to not question what we are told. "Clearly, scientists are much smarter than common people, so they must know better; what they say must be right." "The doctor tells me I have this illness; I have to follow their advice." "Thousands of other people are running their businesses the same way that I am; obviously, this must be the best way."

These are the unspoken rules in our homes, in our schools, in our companies, and in our society. As consumers of products and information, we have been taught not to challenge "the facts." We say that we value curiosity, but our approach to education, work, and culture conditions us not to challenge "the experts."

Tell us what to think, give us a statistic, put it in writing, and most will accept it as true. It is not my poor trigonometry teacher's fault she was not prepared to offer a good explanation. She had never been encouraged to question "the facts," so how could she explain them to twelve-year-olds who had not learned better yet?

If our education environment discourages challenges to intellectual authority, our workplaces are downright draconian. The worker bees are not supposed to process any information beyond the parameters of their job description. A few managers at the top process the data, and then disperse orders: "This is the way we're going to do it, so quit pestering me!"

In Pursuit of Meaning

If you have ever spent thirty minutes with an "inquisitive" toddler—that is, a kid who never stops asking, "Why?"—you understand that this, the most important of all questions, eventually arrives at the limit of human knowledge. After exhausting the line of inquiry, we are left with only three possible responses:

1. Because God/aliens/Mother Nature made it that way.

2. I don't know.

3. It doesn't matter.

This has been the limits of market research, too. Serious researchers understand that historically, causation has been near impossible to demonstrate (and certainly too strong a term to risk their reputation and income on). But the market researcher of tomorrow will be far different from any we have encountered to date. Future generations will have data and technology at their fingertips that allow them to pursue the question of why to the doorway of the three penultimate answers, and perhaps even a few footsteps inside.

Why?

This simple word represents the most primal of self-preservation mechanisms: cause and effect. As children, we may not understand much, but we quickly make the connection between touching a hot surface and pain. It is an evolutionary necessity: cavemen who made the connection between certain plants and sickness learned to avoid them, living longer and having more kids; their unlucky peers died off early. It is a prerequisite for business: we cannot predict the future, so we experiment on a lot of things and go with what works. As Nietzsche would put it: "What doesn't kill us makes us stronger."

Unfortunately, Nietzsche's belief that experience builds knowledge that leads us to be better at making choices in the future is only part of the solution. The truth is that if you make business decisions solely under this belief system, you will eventually experiment with something that outwits you. Sooner or later, your choices will lead you to a point of no return. To truly succeed in business, the questions of how to generate profits must be looked at in context. The circumstances of product applicability, market environment, and more must be a part of your business equation.

SEE THE BIGGER PICTURE

When we sit down with friends or family to talk about life, we often hear, in sometimes agonizing detail, how every decision that has been made led them to their current situation. People tend to reflect on everything from the girlfriend who dumped them leading to a new city of opportunity, to the boss who fired them for dancing on tables at the holiday party. They look deeply at the context of their personal lives and historical choices in their search of meaning.

Yet in the business world, these same people often abandon that wonderful, rich, reflective thought process for a rapid, immediate, fire-from-the-hip type of decision making. It is infuriating that they clearly know how to be contextual thinkers but, for whatever reason, refuse to take that mindset into their professional lives.

Our brains know what is best for us. They are always working towards improving our ability to contextualize information for future decision making. Yet, when it comes to how data, information and market research are used in organizations, most companies are struggling amid the challenges we have explored: politics, lack of data appreciation, insufficient data variety to provide a full picture, or technology too difficult to leverage.

Listen, I do not personally know anyone in the paperclip business. I don't need to know anyone who makes these small wonders of extruded, twisted metal to know that someone, at this very moment, is trying to figure out how they can get more people to buy their product.

If they had access to a contextual analytics solution right now, what would they be looking at?

There would be subjective data on how people consume paperclips: how they are used compared to staples and three-ring binders; the emergency Christmas tree ornament hanger or handy tool for pressing reset buttons on wireless routers or accessing SIM cards. There would be supply chain data covering everything from the price of metal commodities, to how many units were sold at a local store yesterday. There would be discovery information: marketing spend, retail promotions, website traffic, coupon redemptions. Their tools would let them visualize and extract the data instantly by territory, by metal type, by size of box, or by shape of clip. So much information at hand that is actionable, insightful, and contextual.

So what is *your* paperclip?

Do you make cars or canoes?

Pharmaceuticals or farm fertilizer?

Dog food or diapers?

Video games or Velcro?

Whatever your product, technology, or service, the information that will determine whether your business flourishes or flounders is available to you.

Do me a favor: go ahead and put a billion dollar paperclip on your desk.

Before you approve that next research request, buy that next data feed, license a new technology, or green light that new product, look at that paperclip and ask yourself some of the questions we have explored in this book. Evolve beyond corporate myopia to see the bigger picture and think smarter about your data.

AUTHOR'S NOTE

First and foremost, I need to thank my wife Patricia who continues to be everything a husband could ask for in her love and support. I also need to thank my editor Derek Lewis for his patience and honesty, and all those who helped with manuscript readings and provided feedback during the writing process.

My intent with *The Billion Dollar Paperclip* was not only to provide a foundation for those seeking to create a contextual analytics framework, but also to give a little inspiration (in my mind at least).

My hope is that after reading this book you are empowered to think more deeply on the context that surrounds each data point you work with, or are presented with, in the course of doing business. At the very least, if you engage in discussions that examine data by its different types, collection methodologies, and technology utilizations, then you will be on the path to extracting the full potential value from the research you are either creating, buying, or consuming.

I wish you all the best in your business endeavors,

Gregory Short

RESOURCES

Given the evolving state of contextual analysis, rather than provide a static list of resources, books, companies, and people, I encourage you to follow me on twitter **@GregoryShort** where I frequently post links to interesting data, technology or service information relevant to contextual analytics or market research.

You can also reach me directly via **www.GregoryShort.com** with any questions you might have about the book or if you are looking for assistance with developing a contextual data ecosystem within your organization.

ABOUT THE AUTHOR

A serial entrepreneur, Gregory Short has founded two of the most revolutionary market research companies in the world: EEDAR the first company to ever produce a complete contextual analytics framework, and DataDNA, a global leader in data synthesis architecture and information auditing services.

Known for helping clients solve their most challenging data problems, Mr. Short has elevated the market research industry across numerous verticals by establishing partnerships with otherwise competitive vendors to deliver unparalleled value to their mutual clients.

Mr. Short is a pioneer in information management; a thought-leader in data auditing and data synthesis; an internationally recognized expert on research and technology, holding numerous related patents; a frequent speaker at major conferences; a guest lecturer for educational bodies including USC, and SMU; and is active as both a business advisor and board director.

After graduating with a degree in law from Australia, Greg moved to Southern California where he now lives with his family.